How to Trave Live with No Regrets. Learn How to Travel for Free, Find Cheap Places to Travel, and Discover Life-Changing Travel Destinations.

By Dr. Ernesto Martinez

Also by Dr. Ernesto Martinez

How to Travel the World and Live with No Regrets.
Learn How to Travel for Free, Find Cheap Places to Travel, and Discover Life-Changing Travel Destinations.

How to Boost Your Credit Score Range and Make Money with Credit Cards.
How to Repair Your Credit with Credit Repair Strategies.

How to Become Rich and Successful: Creative Ways to Make Money with a Side Hustle
How to Become a Millionaire: Learn the Best Passive Income Ideas

How to Heal Broken Bones Faster. Bone Fracture Healing Tips.
Learn About Bone Fracture Healing Foods, Types of Bone Fractures, and the Five Stages of Bone Healing.

How to Become Rich and Successful. The Secret of Success and the Habits of Successful People.
Entrepreneurship and Developing Entrepreneur Characteristics

How to Lose Weight Without Dieting or Exercise.
Over 250 Ways.
Learn About Foods that Burn Fat, Weight Loss Diets, Weight Loss Tips, Weight Loss Foods, and How to Lose Belly Fat

Cracking the Vitamin Code
How to Build your Own Supplement Stack. The Secret of Stacking Supplements for Beginners, How to Buy Vitamins and Minerals, and the Benefits of Dietary Supplements.

The Hardcore Program
How to build world-class habits and routines. Proven strategies for weight loss, success, and optimal health. How to form yourself into a new you through ritual and routine optimization.

The Adventure Continues: Scan Here

Attaboy Cowboy Health

Attaboy Cowboy Finance

Attaboy Cowboy Finanzas

Attaboy Cowboy Salud

DEDICATION

To my mom and dad, the yin and yang in my life. My mom a fearless woman, who does not know the meaning of failure. My dad who dedicated his life to serving others and taught me to do the same.

Table of contents

Chapter 1.

Introduction

Sometimes, what people want is an escape from their everyday lives. They're not sure how, but they know they want to live a different life, gain new experiences or simply change things up.

It was New Year's Eve 2002 when I ended up in Rome just five hours before the ball dropped at midnight. I had nowhere to stay and no plans for the evening other than to find a warm bed. I walked door to door inquiring at every hostel if they had a room for me. One after another, they turned me down. As I was getting turned away from my eighth hostel, a young American woman named Jennifer spoke up and said I could share her room with her. I was so grateful as it was a cold night, and I was tired from traveling for several days and walking for hours. We ended up traveling together and learning some valuable lessons on resetting life.

Jennifer was from Texas and was in her early 30s. She'd had the same job for over ten years, had always lived in the same town, and had a long-term relationship that was not fulfilling; it was time for a change. So she quit her job, broke up with her boyfriend, gave up her apartment, sold all her belongings, got breast implants, bought some travel gear, and left for a gap year. I was lucky enough to have the opportunity to hear about her renewed interest in life, her big plans, her optimism, and her fresh clarity and purpose for being.

If there is one thing, I've learned about traveling the world, it's this: wherever you find yourself, people are always good. Once you have faith in the goodness of people, the world as a whole becomes an endless open invitation where adventure is second only to your imagination. Put yourself in different worlds and allow those worlds to expand everything that is you.

Although I had started my travels many years before I met Jennifer, she helped open my eyes to the reality that not everyone knows how to execute long-term travel. Most of us believe money is our primary barrier to seeing the world. In fact, it is we ourselves who keep us from seeing everything this beautiful planet has to offer. In the developed world, workers in most European countries, Australia and New Zealand can enjoy four to six weeks off. In the USA and Japan, we average only 1-2 weeks of vacation a year.

In the rest of the world, which is coincidentally where most of the budget travel spots are, people don't always have the luxury of traveling or even time off from work. The majority of them are working as much as they can just to survive or to keep up with the image that Hollywood has given them of a luxurious world that Westerners live in.

I grew up thinking that you had to let it all out when you travel and that spending more than you could afford was the only way to ensure you had a good time. In the US, we save the whole year so we can blow a lot of money on a two-week vacation somewhere close like the Caribbean, Las Vegas, Florida, or California. With only 1-2 weeks, who wants to fly to another continent and suffer for the few days you'll stay there? Instead, most of us opt to spend a lot of money for security, comfort, and familiarity.

Now don't get me wrong, I grew up in Southern California; I know visiting Disneyland or Universal Studios is an experience like no other. However, it sets the tone for what people think traveling is all about, and if you don't have a lot of money, most people think you should just stay at home.

This past summer, I had my cousin and his family from Liberty, Kansas, visit Los Angeles for seven days. My cousin works hard in the oil fields under the scorching sun in the summer and freezing snow in the winter; he even has to deal with occasional tornadoes. He saved all year to give his family the vacation of a lifetime. After the trip, he told me he needed a vacation from this vacation because he was exhausted from walking the streets of Hollywood and sunbathing in Malibu. I laughed, because I thought he was kidding until he confided that he had spent almost $10,000 on the trip, which added up to about $1,600 per person. He said he would have to save up again for another two years to be able to afford a trip like this one. I started doing some numbers and calculated that I spent about $2,000 for four months of travel in Southeast Asia, $2,500 for two months in Europe, $900 for three months in Mexico, and $2,000 for two months in Africa. Someone could travel for a year around the world for what they spent in one week in Southern California.

My cousin, like most people, bought a travel package from one of the companies that did the most marketing. Places like Laos or Namibia don't have the marketing budgets that Hollywood and Disneyland have. As a result, most people don't know how affordable and fascinating it is to visit those countries.

What I realized is that most of us don't know that the rest of the world is a travel bargain and that we can go to most places for much less money and for much longer. Whether you're buying a plane ticket or a new cell phone, it's always smart to shop around and get the best price for the same item or experience.

The idea of seeing wild rhinos roaming the savanna or boating down the Amazon River seems like a pipe dream to most people, but they don't have to be. If you're open to learning some new strategies, you can travel in comfort and not have to miss out on activities to save money. When I go, my goal is to vacation as long as I can for as little as I possible, but I never pass up travel experiences because of the price. Price is relative, and once you've lived your life and passed on, it won't matter how much you spent on your travel memories.

Traveling somewhere new can elicit fear that requires a commitment to overcome and proceed with a new experience. In psychology, there is a term coined Normalcy Bias. It's a belief that things will always function the way

3

things usually have functioned. Traveling challenges you to face new things every day: foods, sounds, people, customs, and the environment. This idea of having to deal with something new causes fear and ultimately shuts most people out of exploring the world.

As I begin writing this book, I am sitting on a sofa inside a bar in Suriname, South America. I had just survived a near-fatal accident in Los Angeles; I'm on crutches, and I'm putting together all my funds so I can travel the world and use my training as an occupational therapist and a naturopathic doctor to rehabilitate myself through travel. After having four operations, being told I would spend six months in bed, and two years in a wheelchair, I was ready to go and see things I may not have been able to see had I not survived.

This is the 90th country that I have visited. By the end of this book, I will be in country number 112. This book has been written throughout the course of my travels, covering the USA, Mexico, Trinidad and Tobago, Guyana, Germany, Dominican Republic, Suriname, Haiti, French Guiana, Costa Rica, Colombia, Venezuela, Denmark, Iceland, Sweden, Norway, Finland, Lithuania, Poland, Czech Republic, Slovakia, Latvia, Estonia, Egypt, Kenya, Ethiopia, Tanzania, Korea, China, and Saipan.

This book will help you travel as easily as possible, to give you an unforgettable experience, and allow you to write your own history. This book will teach you how to look past the expensive travel advertisements and tour company commercials, to travel on your own at a fraction of the cost without missing out on anything. You will learn how to tour as the locals do and have the full experience of adventure, safely, ensuring an unforgettable experience whether you're alone or with others, and finding yourself, all while avoiding the pitfalls that most often ensnare other travelers.

Chapter 2.

Top 5 Excuses Not to Travel that Must Be Conquered

1. If you don't speak the native language, you'll end up starving, homeless, and suffering anywhere outside your country.

I can remember meeting a friend from Los Angeles in Spain who was bilingual in English and Spanish but refused to leave Spain to explore the rest of Europe because he did not speak the language. He ended up staying behind in Spain, while I traveled to Italy and on to the rest of Europe for a few months

Almost every city in the world and every major tourist destination has English-speaking people working at visitor centers. English is the universal language, and people around the world want to cash in on opportunities to work and travel abroad. Without English, you'd be very limited, no matter where you go, whether it's for travel or for work. The internet and globalization have helped to speed up this process of making English the world language.

Remember, there are 8 billion people on this planet. Tourism is a business, and people everywhere depend on it for income. So wherever you may think of visiting, there is already an infrastructure in place for travelers.

People can now communicate seamlessly using technology such as Google Translate or Duolingo. For example, while in Italy, I shared a bunk bed and hung out with a 14-year-old boy from Japan for a few days. His family was wealthy, and both of his parents were college professors. The boy had never studied English before, yet his parents decided it was vital for him to learn. So, his parents sent him backpacking alone for three months across several continents for a crash course in English. He was brilliant and mature for a 14-year-old, something I'm sure developed from traveling alone. After a month of traveling, his conversational English had grown enough for him to carry on conversations with me. What a brilliant plan. Can you imagine the impact this trip would have on someone's life!

2. Foreigners hate me for my race, religion, or nationality.

A Jewish friend of mine was afraid to travel through Mexico with me because he was an Orthodox Jew; he thought people would not accept him. The truth is most people have their own lives to worry about and are not going to waste their time trying to make you feel unwelcome. He ended up going on the trip and had the journey of his life.

During President George Bush's term, several of my American friends would not travel abroad with me, because they were worried about backlash due to the unpopular Iraq War. I even met Americans abroad who would claim they were Canadian to deflect any ill will. I've traveled all around the world through the worst and the best of times, and I've never hidden who I am, and I've never had a problem.

Ignorance is everywhere in the world, so don't add to it. There is always going to be someone who is angry at their situation and wants to take it out on someone else. This should not deter you; this is everyone's planet, and it's here for us to share. I am a Los Angeles Lakers basketball fan. Does that mean I should not attend a Golden State Warriors game?

I always treat people with courtesy and respect, and they treat me equally. It's the same everywhere; if you find that people are not friendly to you, then maybe you need to be nicer. In the end, remember wherever you go, you can always go back home if you're not comfortable wherever you are.

3. Everything is expensive when you travel.

You're going to have tradeoffs everywhere you travel in the world. Let's compare two cities, such as Washington D.C. and Paris. In Washington D.C., most of the best museums, like the Smithsonian, and monuments, like the Lincoln Memorial, are free. However, in Paris, the Louvre is around twenty dollars, and most of the top museums charge an entrance fee. If you want to go to the top of the Eiffel Tower, it costs about thirty dollars, but the wine, baguettes, and art are going to be the best in the world and at the best prices. The subway system is also much easier to use and more affordable.

No matter where you're going, you will be spending money on things you usually wouldn't. That's part of the travel experience. You're paying to see something new, like going to the movies to see the latest blockbuster or buying a meal at the new restaurant down the street.

The flight is usually the biggest expense, but you can make it up in other ways during your trip. You can save on accommodations, food, alcohol, and entertainment. If you make adjustments, you can live the same anywhere you go. In the Czech Republic, the beer is some of the best in the world, and it's cheaper than water. I ate a lot of eggs, dairy, and bread as they were very inexpensive there. When I traveled to Greece, those same food items were expensive, but olives, cheese, and tomatoes were a good deal. So I changed my diet and ate what the locals did.

Try to live as much like the locals as you can; this will give you a better experience and save you money. Avoid hotels and use Craigslist to find rooms or apartments for rent at a much lower price than even Airbnb. As you interact with locals, ask them where the best places are to eat and visit. These places are usually less expensive and give you a more traditional experience. Use the bus or ride the subway instead of taking Uber.

One more thing to keep in mind is that traveling is usually cheaper than staying at home. When I calculate my rent ($1,500), food ($400), car ($300 gas only), and all my other expenses, I usually end up paying around $2,800 per month, and that only covers my basic living expenses. I have never spent more than that amount for a month's worth of travel. I know that it can be done very quickly, even if you don't make an effort to save on your trip. But I am not trying to spend all my hard-earned money in one place. I'm trying to make the most of it, and enjoy it as much as I can. For some useful strategies to build income for traveling; check out the books: How to Become Rich and Successful. The Secret of Success and the Habits of Successful People or How to Become Rich and Successful: Creative Ways to Make Money with a Side Hustle.

4. You'll miss out on activities with family and friends at home.

Sure, you'll miss out on some activities or events at home, but you'll be making your own experiences abroad. When you're back in town, you'll have a lot more stories and experiences to share with everyone. Plus, you can always make video calls or send videos of you singing happy birthday. Those tend to be unforgettable.

5. What if I get sick or something happens to me while I'm traveling?

Healthcare is inexpensive everywhere in the world, except in the USA. My healthcare premium is $400 a month. When I travel, I buy travel health insurance for $56 a month with better coverage, including a medevac plane back to the USA from anywhere on the planet. So it's much cheaper to get insured and have medical treatment anywhere outside the USA.

One of my friends went to Spain for the running of the bulls and broke her hip. She ended up needing hip surgery and was hospitalized for two weeks. When she got out of the hospital, she was worried about the medical bills, but was billed only $80 for everything.

My 84-year-old aunt Delia and her 68-year-old boyfriend

Oscar wanted to go to Argentina, so her boyfriend could visit his 94-year-old mom after not seeing her for 40 years. Their main concern was, "what if we get sick and die?" My response was, "Even more reason to go." Carpe diem, getting sick and dying is more reason to travel and do what you've dreamed of. You're never too old to travel. You don't want to go out with regrets.

As for crime and terrorism, worrying unnecessarily about that is what keeps most people from traveling. Unfortunately, after the attacks on September 11, television ratings went through the roof as people were glued to their TVs, hoping to get information that would keep them safe. The news channels caught on and started using fear to keep people watching TV, watching commercials, and generating more revenue for the networks.

I remember watching the news and listening to the weather forecaster predicting rain. Those days are gone. Now we keep hearing a "storm" is coming. It's the same thing but rebranded into something that will catch your attention much more and cause you to stay glued to the TV to help boost the television station's ratings.

When you turn on the news, sure you'll see some bad news; that's what sells. But then again there are 8 billion of us, and things are going to happen, and they happen everywhere just the same. Don't be fooled by the overgeneralization that the world is unsafe; it's just the opposite.

Chapter 3.

Top 5 Personality Traits of a Successful Traveler

1. Be Courageous

Do you remember the anxiety you felt on your first day of kindergarten, high school, college, getting ready to walk the stage at graduation, the day of your wedding, taking your final exams, or having a job interview? You had to conquer that feeling and move from one phase of your life on to the next. Life is a series of experiences, one greater than the other, and as you master them, your life only gets better. Starting out on a new journey can be just as stressful and just as life-changing. Whether you're packing your bags to drive cross country and start a new life in the Golden State of California, immigrating to a new country to live in a new culture and a new language, or making the decision to use your yearly two-week vacation to set yourself straight and get you on the path you have always wanted in life. Traveling is man's way of satisfying a curious mind and understanding why we are here. It gives you the chance to reset your life.

Taking that first step is the hardest, but once you've made it, you'll never look back, and the future will always be brighter for the courage you showed today.

When I was sixteen, my friends invited me to Atlanta, Georgia, to the most prominent baseball card collector's event of the year: "The National." Unfortunately, I only had enough money to buy a round-trip plane ticket and have twenty dollars left over for the weeklong trip. Fortunately, my friend David (also sixteen), Nestor (fifteen) and I, all decided to go anyway. This trip laid the foundation for what has been an exciting life full of travels while learning fundamental survival techniques.

First off, we had to find shelter. Luckily Atlanta has temperatures in the 90s at night in the summertime so we simply slept in the park on the lush, soft Southern grass. As for food, we found a taco place at the Convention Center that had a free salsa bar. So every day, I purchased a taco and then loaded the plate with lettuce and salsas, making a large filling taco salad. As the days went on, we discovered the Salvation Army, which offered a large bowl of chili beans, bread, and all-you-can-drink Kool-Aid for just fifty cents. We then learned how to use the bus and the subway. We also learned how to hustle making money, selling baseball cards, and use the money to go sightseeing. These experiences helped me develop my skills in negotiation and survival for my future business and academic endeavors.

One of the greatest achievements of your life will be to overcome your fears by starving them and feeding your opportunities instead.

2. Be Flexible

When you're traveling, things rarely go as planned, so expect the unexpected and have fun with the surprises that await you. It can be difficult and disappointing to let go of plans, not knowing if you'll have the chance to attempt your journey again. Especially if you have spent a lot of money, traveled a long way, made a lot of adjustments to go on this trip, or dreamed of having this experience for a long time. But, the more flexible you can be with your travel plans, the more options will open up for you, the more money you'll save, the further you'll travel, and the more fun you'll have along the way. The most exciting times in your life will be the ones you least expect.

3. Be Curious, Just Go

If you have a burning desire to explore the world, or even just to see one place you've always been curious about, then start focusing your energy on that goal and go! Don't wait for a better time. Just do it, or you will regret it when you are too old or too caught up in your life to travel. If you can't find a travel partner, go solo.

Traveling alone is a unique experience in self-discovery, and it gives you a chance to really immerse yourself in the travel experience. It allows you to see, hear, taste, smell, and touch a new environment without being filtered by your travel partner's ideas.

I was once sitting in a café having a drink in the middle of the day in New Delhi, India. The streets were full of people. Two young men about fifteen years old walked up barefoot wearing loincloths. Suddenly, one of them pulled down his loincloth and squatted on the sidewalk. He then started defecating as he kept on talking to his friend. Once he finished, he stood up, sliding his loincloth back up, and continued the conversation as if nothing had happened.

Meanwhile, the crowds of people just walked around them as if nothing was happening. No one batted an eye, and it just happened as if it was the inconsequential act it indeed was. Had I been at home in the USA or with a fellow American, the incident would have elicited an adverse reaction. These responses have developed since childhood and are influenced by our culture, family, education, socioeconomic levels, and even the environment we live in.

These responses sometimes force you to judge and experience things in a way that allows you to relate them to experiences that you had in your life to help you normalize and categorize experiences into something easier to understand. These types of conditioned responses allow you to process life. They give you comfort and prevent you from being scared by new experiences. However, they also limit your ability to experience things from a different perspective. They prevent your brain from developing new tools for seeing and understanding the world and the people in it. That's sometimes why we humans seek to dissociate or dehumanize people for being different from us or for holding different views from ours.

Traveling with someone familiar to you can be comforting, but it can also remind you of who you are and who you are supposed to be, which allows for little in terms of change and development as a person. Traveling alone can take practice, but as you develop the skill, you learn to let go of who you are, and you learn how you can become the person you want to be by social referencing the skills, abilities, social norms, and knowledge of other people.

Traveling alone will teach you a variety of social tools to use in your work and personal life. You'll learn how to be open-minded, accept things for what they are, and avoid judging or changing them. This will allow you to flow better and be successful in your personal and business life. Remember that we always want to be around people who understand us and who make us feel comfortable. The better you are at understanding and accepting people, the more successful and happier you will be.

4. Be Patient

Travel is exciting, but that doesn't mean it's always easy or that you won't run into issues occasionally. Adverse life experiences are just part of life, and you need to be patient when necessary, never losing your temper or being unrealistic. You may have to wait for hours for documents in lines or going through immigration. Missing flights, boats, trains and buses should be expected. Your patience will be tested during some of the most unique experiences you'll ever have, and that is why patience is an essential personality trait for any great traveler. Being patient allows you to be a better person, have better mental and physical health, which makes it easier to achieve goals. When you are patient, you'll have the advantage of being in a better position to respond to situations once things calm down.

Live without Regrets

In my practice as an occupational therapist and a naturopathic doctor, I have had the opportunity to learn from many people who have passed on. While standing at people's bedsides as they prepare to transition, they often share their last, most meaningful, and unfiltered thoughts on life. It's at this moment that people will often realize they don't have to be anyone in particular. They don't have to worry about upsetting anyone. They can unburden themselves of thoughts and feelings, without considering the consequences of doing so.

Believe it or not, about half the people I see pass on without a loved one by their side. In their final moments, people often sum their life up in terms of achievements, most importantly, the places they visited in the world. In some cases, I've had the opportunity to stand by and accompany them while listening to their final words; including hearing about their regrets, estranged family, not living the life they would have wanted to live, or not traveling as much as they would have liked.

The reasons are familiar: making decisions to satisfy other people instead of yourself or being scared to act on your dreams. Traveling is relative as some people tell me they have visited a lot of places, and when I ask where they've been, they'll list a few places within a few hours of Los Angeles. Then there are those who don't feel satisfied even though they've traveled to most continents of the world.

Therefore, traveling is subjective, every person has their own idea of what it means and how many places one must visit to be well-traveled. What's important is that you achieve what you desire and that you feel fulfilled with what you have accomplished.

How many dying people have I met in hospitals who regretted traveling? Not one! Working with people who are sick and dying allows you to learn from their knowledge and unique experiences. It enables you to ask yourself, "Do I want to go out with regrets?" No way! Be patient, and slow down.

5. Perseverance

It takes perseverance to make our travel and life dream a reality in the first place. It's tempting to give up when seemingly impossible odds begin to stack up, but you have to push through, even when your plans may seem out of your reach. Things always work out as they should if you're tenacious.

My older brother Bobby and I planned several trips together. Although he enjoyed traveling and longed to see as many places as he could, he lived as if he had all the time in the world. On several occasions, he would tell me on the day of departure, "Go on without me, and I'll fly in tomorrow and meet you there." We would be in daily contact, and he would say things like, "OK, I'll be flying in tomorrow at 3 pm," and each day he would push the date out further.

I continued my adventures while holding on to hope that he would eventually make the trip. Most of the time he wouldn't make it because he claimed, "Baby, I just have too many bills to pay," and I would respond, "Bobby, your bills are always going to be there, but you won't always have the opportunity to travel." Then, at the age of thirty-two, my brother was lying in a hospital bed in the intensive care unit (ICU) very sick with AIDS, faced with the prospect that he was close to the end.

I faithfully stood by his side for several months preparing meal plans, supplements, alternative treatments, and reassuring him that all would be okay. One of the strategies for healing we implemented was visualization. The invisible world creates the visible world around you. So, we covered his walls in pictures of unique destinations from around the world. In hopes of encouraging his mind to heal his body so he could persevere and achieve his dreams of seeing more of the world.

One day, feeling exhausted from the fight for his life, he gazed up at me, holding my hand. He looked into my eyes and cried as he told me: "Baby, you are the best brother ever. Thank you for everything you do for every one of us. You're always thinking about us and how to help us. I should have listened to you when you tried to get me to go on trips with you. Instead, I wasted all my time working, just to pay for all this stuff, and now I'm going to die. You told me that my bills would always be there, and I could pay them later. But I didn't listen, and now I'm going to die." Then he started crying as he held my hand and begged, "Baby, I don't want to die. I'm not ready yet," and I reassured him, "You're not going to die. You'll be okay." Within a few weeks, he died, and his opportunity to live the life and have the experiences he wanted expired with him for now. If you don't act, your time will expire, whether you're ready or not, and you will never know the life you could have lived.

I never gave up hope of taking trips with my brother, and even though we didn't make some of our journeys together, we did have the chance to form some of the most unforgettable experiences of my life. I look back with joy, knowing I acted with determination to achieve my goals of having some unique travel experiences with my brother.

Life is about moments. (My brother Bobby is on the right, and his boyfriend David is on the left.) Don't wait for them. Create them.

Chapter 4.

Packing Tips

Top 5 Travel Packing Hacks: How to Pack Light

African Safari in Tanzania

There are two types of travelers, those who pack light and those who wish they had packed light. Think things through, pack carefully, organize, and you'll be able to leave on a two-week vacation with a small duffel bag and a shoulder bag; or my favorite option, one backpack, and no checked baggage.

1. Security

The less you hand over to others to handle for you, the fewer issues related to theft, damage, or misrouting you're going to have. The more bags you carry, the more risk of airline staff or other passengers taking items out of your pockets, bed bugs or other parasites hitching a ride home with you, or even having your belongings destroyed by weather.

On a trip to South America, the airline lost my bags. I called phone numbers, mailed in paperwork, and never received any compensation or acknowledgment of my items being lost. Everyone wants to feel safe about packing their valuables and loading them into a plane, but the reality is that human error exists, and inevitably, your bags may get lost. The experience can really ruin a pre or post-trip experience. In most cases, you have almost no recourse.

After that experience, I tried travel insurance and coincidentally lost more luggage. I was asked to fill out lots of paperwork and provide itemized receipts of the items in my bags. I did not have the original store receipts for the things I purchased, so I received no reimbursement.

If you'd like to have the opportunity to pick through and buy items that other people have lost with their luggage, check out the Unclaimed Baggage Center (unclaimedbaggage.com), which is located in Scottsboro, Alabama. They specialize in selling unclaimed or lost items from airports.

2. Save Money

Make traveling more accessible by cutting your costs. You can avoid checked baggage fees, excess baggage weight fees, carts to haul your stuff around, and paying porters. It'll be easier for you to take public transportation (like airport personnel does), rather than shuttles, limos, Uber, and (scam-prone) taxis. Or, you can just walk and enjoy having more contact with locals.

I recently booked a trip through a budget airline from Los Angeles, California; to Reykjavik, Iceland; to Stockholm, Sweden; back to Reykjavik, and then back to Los Angeles. The flight should have cost over $2,000, but I paid only $350 with taxes and fees included. The only catch was that I could not check any bags, and if I did, I would have had to pay $50 per pack per each segment of the flight. Therefore, had I checked my backpack; I would have had to pay $200 extra to transport it on four parts of flights. If I were to check two bags, I would have been paying more in bags than I did for my entire trip.

If you're traveling somewhere where the weather is cold, then you will need to bring high-quality and lightweight clothing for cold weather. To avoid the baggage fee, I wore my clothes three layers thick. I removed the metal support bars from my backpack, so I could fold it up and fit it into the sample carry-on luggage bin. Once on the plane, you can remove the extra clothes, put them back into your backpack, and place it in the overhead bin.

3. Mobility

Less stuff means greater mobility, faster online check-in; you don't have to arrive early to check your luggage, and you get to avoid waiting in line at the check-in counter. If you miss a flight, it's delayed, wish to be switched to an earlier flight, or a seat opens up on standby, you're going to have more options since you're not constrained by luggage. If you have luggage, you're going to have fewer of these opportunities, because most of the time there is not enough time to find your bags.

When you arrive at your destination without a bunch of bags, you can just get off the plane, go without having to wait in baggage claim, avoid having to wait in line for customs, and be the first to leave the airport. With one bag carrying only necessities, you will have less luggage to lug around and less chance of your luggage getting lost, damaged or stolen in transit. Occasionally the plane may be oversold and you'll have the opportunity to sell your airplane seat by volunteering to be "bumped" on full flights, or you can travel for free as an air courier.

Once you leave the airport, you can board trains, trams, and buses with ease. If you don't like your hotel, you can walk down the street and find a better one at a lower price without the pressure of dragging all your bags around.

4. Tranquility

Luggage is baggage, the more you pack, the more it will weigh you down physically and mentally. Packing less will save you the energy that you don't have to expend packing and hauling items around. You'll be able to relax your mind, always knowing where your stuff is, not having to spend extra time packing, not having to worry about someone taking your stuff, or leaving it behind, because everything will be with you. Going to a new place can be challenging as you try to figure out an unfamiliar environment. A person who packs less will have fewer unnecessary things to worry about, and more time to focus on having fun traveling.

On a return trip from Peru, I was told I had too many carry-on items, so I started stuffing my checked luggage with carry-on items to save on fees, and the airline staff commented on how beautiful my souvenirs were. When I arrived back in Los Angeles, all of my souvenirs had been plucked from my bags despite my having TSA approved locks on them! The locks had been opened, and after my souvenirs were stolen, they were closed again. This means it was an airport worker who took my stuff. I had some souvenirs that I was very excited about bringing home and losing them was really upsetting. But the experience reminded me that the material things I bring back from trips are not essential and can be easily damaged or stolen anywhere. You're better off not expanding the time and effort on carrying material things around. Instead, enjoy the experience, rest your mind, and bring home the memories instead.

Traveling light allows you to focus your mind on your spiritual development and thinking about what's essential in your life.

5. Environment

One of the most enormous benefits of traveling light are the benefits to the planet. When you're buying, consuming, and transporting around less stuff, it's going to require less fuel, create less trash, and do less damage to the environment. The more environmentally responsible you are, the better off the planet is going to be for everyone to enjoy, now and in the future. Air travel causes significant damage to the environment; make up for part of it by following some of the guidelines at the end of this book on ten ways to decrease your impact on the environment. While exploring nature, don't collect rocks, shells, seeds, animals, or anything else as you can be spreading disease to other areas. Stay on hiking trails, as wandering off can cause soil erosion and damage the surrounding environment.

While traveling in southern Mexico, Africa, South America and Asia, you can see the rainforest being slashed and burned in front of your eyes every day. One year, I went to Chiapas in southern Mexico and had to drive six hours through lush jungle to reach the pyramids. Two years later I returned, and the drive had been reduced to three hours. A large portion of the forest had been replaced with palm oil plantations. This was a shocking reminder of how fast the world is changing because of human activity. If you spend much time in the great outdoors, follow the Leave No Trace principles; it's the best practice we should follow to enjoy and protect our natural spaces.

We all impact this earth, just try to minimize it as much as you can. The clothes I bring with me on my trips are usually from thrift stores. The money you spend in thrift stores goes to helping and rehabilitating disabled people. The clothes themselves can be used as gifts for homeless people or for those whom I see committing random acts of kindness.

Backpack or Suitcase

There are several factors to consider when choosing how to transport your items. Backpacks are recommended for most types of traveling as they are easier to carry, lightweight, and safer.

Pulling a suitcase with wheels can be difficult on uneven

surfaces, curbs, cobblestone streets, and stairs, and it also puts you at risk for hurting your neck, back and shoulders as you're forced to move the suitcase with your shoulder hyperextended behind you with only one half of your body. Also, when lifting the concentrated weight of the bag into a vehicle, upstairs, or onto a higher surface, you'll usually be doing it with one arm and often twisting your body while standing on uneven surfaces. This kind of body position is certain to cause back injury.

We don't think about muscle strain when packing our travel bag, because it's usually resting on another surface. It may not seem very heavy, but once you start lifting, rolling, or carrying it, you're going to get tired and put yourself at risk of hurting yourself.

I had not given much thought to this until I worked at a workplace injury clinic across the street from the Los Angeles International Airport. All my patients worked either at the airport or for the airlines, and business was excellent. We had a long waiting list, the clinic was massive, we had about fifteen therapists, and I treated four patients at the same time. In my twenty years of practice, I've never attended the volume of patients that I saw from such a small population. The patients had every job you could imagine at the airport, but all their injuries were related to baggage. People of all ages and physical conditions would injure their necks, shoulders, wrists, elbows, backs, hips, spine, and knees from simply lifting one piece of luggage the wrong way. Then they'd end up with multiple surgeries and off from work, sometimes for years.

I could see firsthand the damage that luggage can have on the human body. To clarify, it wasn't the luggage exactly, it was the awkward lifting positions, often off-balance, to move something that is a pack of concentrated weight. The more I analyzed it, I'd say that 99% of the activities that people generally engage in are not as unsafe as moving luggage. Biomechanically, another comparable activity would be to move a 40 lb bag of dog food, but that has a very low frequency, since most people buy the food, take it home, and don't repeat the same activity until they run out of it in a few weeks. With luggage, you're going to be doing this several times a day. putting you at high risk of injury.

This is the reason when you go to the airport, you'll notice that the airline check-in agents want you to lift your own luggage onto the scale. Once you board the plane, the flight attendants will not help you lift your luggage into the overhead bin. I've even been asked several times by the stewardess if I'd help a fellow passenger lift and position their luggage in the overhead. The employees are now being taught to handle the passengers' luggage as little as possible, due to the extremely high risk of injury.

With this in mind, I strongly recommend using a lightweight travel backpack. Travel backpacks are made of lighter materials, have a metal frame for equal weight distribution, a lighter, usually weatherproof exterior, and you can add safety locks to protect your belongings.

Use both shoulder and waist straps. This evenly distributes the weight across your body and gives you more power to move, and it's less strain for your joints and reduces the risk of injury. Also, when the weight is on your back, you get to move the weight with your legs and back which have the largest and strongest muscles in your body. When you're carrying a suitcase, you have all the pressure on your fingers, and if you're wheeling it, then the pressure is on your wrist and shoulder carrying the load. There are just too many factors that can cause injury.

Don't sling the backpack over your shoulder. It's recommended that after you load your backpack, sit on your bed, and slide both straps over your shoulders, lean forward, and then stand up. This way you're not twisting your back with a heavy weight on it and risking injury.

Don't carry your backpack with one strap; this causes an unequal weight distribution and puts you at a higher risk of straining your back.

Carrying a backpack also allows you to build your

overall body strength, which will increase your endurance and power while you travel. The more you improve your strength and endurance, the more activities you'll have the ability to participate in.

Increased safety with backpacks in case you have to run or leave somewhere in a hurry. You'll have much more mobility if you have a backpack versus having to run carrying a suitcase or wheeling luggage behind you. You also have less chance of leaving something behind because your backpack is attached to you.

The backpack will save you time with packing; it's easy to find your belongings, and much easier to carry a pack for a prolonged period versus luggage. Many places will also allow you to walk in and look around with a backpack, but they may not let you do so with luggage.

Travel backpacks range in size from 43 to 110 liters. The difference in weight between a large one and a small one is ounces. Therefore, it doesn't make sense to get a smaller one to save on weight, so I recommend getting the biggest pack you could physically handle carrying. If it feels too heavy when you fill it up, then just unload some of your stuff until you're comfortable supporting the weight, but at least you'll have the extra room in case you ever need to carry a few additional items for a short period of time or to condense two bags into one at the airport so you won't be charged an additional baggage fee that can run up to $100 extra. Then, once you get to where you're going, you can unload the gifts or other items you were transporting to your destination.

Although you can order backpacks online, I recommend going into a store to try them on. Backpacks are like shoes, if you don't have a good fit, it's going to start hurting after carrying it for a while. Think of a new pair of shoes that rub you in that one spot and tears your skin, the same happens with backpacks. The best stores to check out are REI, North Face, Columbia, Dicks Sporting Goods, Big 5 Sporting Goods, and any other bag or sporting goods store. The backpacks run from $100 to $1,500. I recommend buying a quality budget backpack and spending your money on traveling instead. I purchased an excellent backpack for $100 that I used for ten years until it was stolen in South Africa.

What Clothes to Bring

This is where you will have to decide what you are comfortable doing without. The primary items you'll be packing are shirts for men and tops for women. These are the items that get most wrinkled, dirty, and sweaty. Everything else can be reused several times if needed. Depending on the weather and temperatures at your destination, you should pick fabrics accordingly. Synthetic fibers won't wrinkle, dry faster, and are best for colder weather. Natural fibers like cotton will wrinkle, but they keep you more relaxed in hot climates. Bring neutral colors so you can blend in, and so you can mix and match clothes easily to make multiple outfits out of a few articles of clothing.

Cold weather is the toughest to pack for because the clothing is thicker and heavier. I suggest investing in one outfit made of high-quality fibers to be used in freezing temperatures. These types of articles last forever, and they are incredibly lightweight. You can find lots of winter clothing at thrift stores since the clothing is seasonal.

I once traveled to the Bolivian Andes during the winter in shorts and sandals, the weather was below zero, and no matter how much money I spent, I could not get good quality clothes to keep me warm. All that I could find were wool socks and sweaters. These are porous, allow all the cold air in, and you lose body heat. I looked like the Michelin man with five sweaters on and yet I was still freezing.

Toiletries

Adhere to the Transportation Security Administration (TSA) guidelines to avoid having your items confiscated and dumped in the trash. You may put any sized bottles of liquid in your checked luggage. In your carry-on luggage, you're limited to one quart-sized plastic bag that can hold multiple bottles with none larger than 3.4 ounces (100ml).

If I'm going to a jungle or a tropical location for an extended period, I'll pack a small bag to check-in for items such as skin lotions, sunblock, and insect repellent. Then I have the brands I prefer and ready to use on arrival. The quality of these products is typically not as good outside industrialized countries, and they charge a premium for them since most of the locals don't usually buy them. Try to pack just enough toiletries for your trip, so you don't have to haul them back or give them away as tips on your way back.

Sample Packing Guide

This is a slimmed-down list of essential items that can fit into a carry-on bag. I highly recommend a travel backpack because of its versatility, light weight, collapsibility, expandability, and many useful pockets with side and top entry.

Absolute Essentials

- Passport
- Driver's license
- Health insurance information (essential phone numbers to call).
- Plane tickets or printouts of boarding passes
- Bank cards (debit and credit) plus some cash in dollars or euros since they are accepted worldwide
- Details of accommodations, transportation, and itinerary (printed or saved on your iPhone)

Clothing

- Hooded jacket - density of jacket depends on climate - or lightweight rain jacket, if hot
- 2-4 t-shirts
- 1 pair of jeans or cargo pants
- 1 pair of dress pants or khakis

- 1 pair of swim shorts/swimsuit
- 3 pairs of socks
- 3 sets of underwear
- 1 sun hat, if visiting sunny climate, or beanie for cold weather
- 1 pair walking shoes/boots - climate-appropriate
- 1 pair of sandals for showers to avoid getting fungus or for everyday use
- 1 pair of dressy shoes - for going out to formal events
- 1 pair of black dress socks
- Belt

How to Pack

Roll your clothes when packing. It prevents wrinkles and allows you to pack more clothes into your bags. Once you roll, you'll wonder why you ever bothered folding. Packing your clothes in Ziploc bags will help prevent wrinkles even more. If you're traveling with a collared shirt, run a belt under the collar before rolling, this will help prevent the collar from wrinkling.

Accessories

- Concealed money pouch
- Dummy wallet filled with low-value currency, soup can labels, and expired credit cards
- Reusable water bottle
- iPhone with charger and headphones
- Nail clippers
- Sunglasses and case
- Earplugs: being able to sleep in a noisy place is invaluable
- Pen and small notepad: details of flights and other vital information are recorded here
- Travel guidebooks, maps, or phrasebooks
- Reading material: at least one paperback book (several more loaded onto my iPhone)
- Universal travel adaptor, if traveling abroad
- Mailing labels save time when filling out forms
- Collapsible duffel bag

- 5 small zip ties
- 5-gallon size Ziploc bags

Optional

- Small first aid kit: usually only taken on activity trips
- Antibacterial hand sanitizer
- Face mask in case of a pandemic

Know the Rules

Know which items not to bring on the plane. This applies to safety, size, weight, and even food, as there are restrictions on all of these.

Safety restrictions vary in different countries but include obvious safety hazards (knives in your carry-on, flammable liquids in any of your luggage), not-so-obvious hazards (nail clippers or files in your carry-on), and a few seemingly inexplicable items such as an unopened bottle of water on US flights, unless you purchased it after going through security.

Weight and size restrictions depending on the airline, so check their website ahead of time for more information. Most medium-sized duffel bags and hand luggage marketed as carry-on will be accepted into the cabin.

Avoid bringing nuts on planes. These can cause allergic reactions in fellow passengers.

Don't bring agricultural items (fruits, vegetables, seeds), meat, or dairy products. Although you may be able to get away with it in some countries, many regulate these items to reduce the spread of non-native species and disease.

Extra Items

Bring one extra shoulder bag to be used as a day bag to carry food, water, or for shopping (so you're not using plastic bags). This bag can also be used to bring souvenirs back home with you.

Do you remember the movie Catch Me If You Can with Leonardo DiCaprio? In the film, Leonardo's character carries a dummy wallet stuffed with labels from tin cans to pose as currency. He gives the wallet to people to hold in case he is robbed, so he can quickly flee the scene. A wallet stuffed with plastic credit card offer cards that often come in the mail, product labels, and low-value currency from other countries with maybe a few US dollars in front. I keep this wallet in my back pocket. In case I am robbed, I hand them this wallet.

I also wear a belt with a looped money pouch I can carry under my pants. I leave a credit card, ID, and cash in my main bag, wherever it's being stored, as a backup if I lose everything on my person.

If you're traveling with a partner, you can also give them access to all your information. Store some cash and credit cards with them, and vice versa.

Two of my favorite pieces of travel equipment are Ziploc bags and zip ties. Use Ziploc bags to waterproof essential papers, your camera, food, dirty clothes, etc. Zip ties can be used for many things, such as fixing broken backpack straps or holding things together. On a trip through southern Africa, the bumper fell off my rental car. I needed to finish my trip and return the vehicle with the bumper, or the rental car company would have charged a lot of money to replace it. I used some zip ties to hold the bumper to the frame until I was ready to return the car a few weeks later.

Backpack locks and/or a wire mesh to put over your backpack to prevent people from getting into your bag if you are traveling through an area with pickpockets or a high crime rate.

For female travelers, if you use tampons, pack some in a Ziploc as some countries do not carry them.

Due to the frequency of having to fill out forms, it's a good idea to bring mailing labels that can be stuck onto forms in place of filling everything out, and a pen that can be used to fill out forms while waiting in lines at customs, border crossings, bus stations, or airports.

There are different plug and outlet types throughout the world, so bring a universal adapter for your electronic devices. I also recommend bringing a car charger and backup chargers in case one gets lost or broken. It can be difficult to find electronic accessories, especially when you are traveling in developing countries. Not having an adapter to charge your electric shaver, laptop, or other cell phones can cause unnecessary problems.

If losing your luggage keeps you up at night. There's a way to safeguard against this scenario using a luggage tracker. There are three types of technology used to track luggage, Bluetooth, GPS, and GSM. Bluetooth works well for shorter distances, like airport terminals, and doesn't require a monthly data plan. Global position system (GPS) trackers use satellite technology to locate a bag's location. While it has coverage worldwide, a disadvantage is that physical barriers, such as buildings, can block the signal. Global system for mobile (GSM) is the world's most extensive digital cellular system; luggage trackers work using cell tower signals, the same as mobile phones. But some countries, particularly those in Asia, don't use GSM. That means trackers need a different SIM card, which may incur extra fees, such as roaming.

Bag and Weight Restrictions

Trains and Cruise Ships

You're limited to two bags weighing less than 50 lbs. each, and no restrictions on liquids. However, these rules are not usually enforced.

Planes

Domestic travel: most airlines now only allow carry-on bags and charge extra for checked luggage up to 50 lbs. each and a surcharge beyond that weight limit.

International travel: most airlines allow one bag, and

some allow two bags up to 50 lbs. each and a surcharge beyond that weight limit.

If I have more luggage than is allowed for free or I think my bag may exceed the allowable weight. I avoid the check-in counter and self-check through the airline's application on my iPhone. Then I wait until everyone else boards the plane for the final boarding call before I board the plane. Being last to board can give you multiple benefits because the airlines must leave on time, or late departures can cause a ripple effect throughout an airline's schedule. If the airline workers see you have too many bags or are overweight, they tend to look the other way because they want to ensure the flight is on time. It also makes it easier for the workers to ignore your bags because there aren't other passengers watching and saying, "hey, why did you charge me and not charge him?" Also, if it turns out it is an oversold flight, you'll be the first to be offered financial incentives to give up your seat for a later flight if you choose. About 90% of the time, this works. When it doesn't, I carry at least one premium credit card that covers a limited amount of luggage fees per year.

Another option is to pack your second bag with your food. In recent years, most airlines have stopped serving food, so it is common for people to carry extra bags with food onto the flight. Most airlines allow only one carry-on bag but do not count bags of food. If I have two bags, I bring a large reusable grocery bag and place my second backpack inside, then on top of that, I carry my food items. No one has ever asked me to look inside my bag since they see it's a grocery bag; they don't count it.

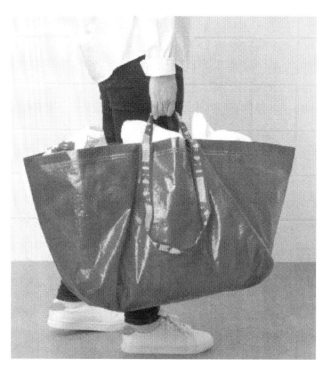

My other favorite strategy is wearing your luggage, a creative yet often overlooked travel hack. Consider this: instead of trying to fit everything into limited bag space, why not utilize the ample room on your person? I've perfected this art over the years. My go-to is an oversized windbreaker – an XL size, even though I typically wear a large. This particular jacket has been customized with additional pockets and is spacious enough to cleverly disguise a backpack slung in front of me, giving the appearance of a protruding belly. The windbreaker's pockets are then systematically filled to the brim.

Hardcore triple pack technique with the same clothes. From left A. Two full bags allowed; one on the back and one in the hand B. No bags allowed; everything packed on your body, even the grocery bag, is empty and can be folded into your pocket. C. One full bag allowed; so, the full grocery bag (Yellow and green bag) can be hidden under your jacket, so only the black bag on your back is visible.

But the windbreaker is just the start. Beneath it, I layer multiple clothing items for added warmth and extra storage. And remember the pants; cargo pants and shorts are a godsend with many pockets for storing additional items. For good measure, I drape a hoodie sweater around my waist, using its pockets as extra storage for things like socks. If I'm feeling particularly audacious, I might tuck a lightweight backpack under my windbreaker on my back. You might think this attracts attention, but in all my travels, I've never been stopped or asked to shed layers. Upon boarding the plane, I quickly shed these multiple layers, ensuring a comfortable flight. Embracing this strategy, I've redefined the meaning of "packing light."

One other benefit of late boarding is it allows you to survey the plane after all other passengers have taken seats for the best-remaining seats so you can upgrade yourself to a more desirable seat, such as having a row to yourself, a seat closer to the front, or an emergency exit with more legroom.

Chapter 5.

Travel Documents

In the Oval Office at the Ronald Regan Library Simi Valley California

Documents

Everywhere you go in the world, you are going to need all or some of the following: vaccination records, passport, business contacts, and plane tickets. Set up two email or cloud accounts with different companies such as Google and Hotmail, because some governments will monitor your email as a condition for entering their country. As a result, some companies have refused this intrusion so you cannot access your accounts in those countries.

If you need to travel to North Korea, Russia, China, Cuba, Ethiopia, Venezuela, or some other country that hinders free speech and internet privacy by blocking access to particular websites, you can download VPN software such as Psiphon for your smartphone, tablet, or computer.

The VPN software allows you to circumvent this type of security and check your email or other internet sites that might be blocked.

Companies like Google and Hotmail don't allow those governments to access your personal information, so the governments have banned access to their servers as a form of censorship. Yahoo accounts are usually accessible to communicate with others while in these countries. It's also a good idea to have two accounts, since sometimes company servers can be down for periods, and you don't have to risk not being able to check your email or access essential travel documents.

Make digital copies by either taking clear photos or scanning vaccination records, passports, business contacts, phonebook contacts, plane tickets, a list of medications, copies of prescriptions for drugs (in case you need a refill), and all other pertinent documents. Store copies of all this information in your two email or cloud accounts. Suppose you get robbed or lose your luggage, how will you get out of or across countries without your documents? This method will allow you to print up copies that are often accepted in most travel outlets and government bodies. E-tickets save money and help you lower the importance of your cargo.

While in South Africa, my car was broken into three separate times, and all my documents were stolen. Fortunately, I had my documents backed up, so I was able to use my digital copies to complete my trip.

In tropical latitudes, such as South America and Africa, where yellow fever is a problem, they will not allow you in unless you have proof of yellow fever vaccinations for fear that you will add to the ongoing problem or spread the disease to other places, making it harder to contain. This helps them protect themselves and you from public health problems pertinent to that area.

Phone contacts, I recommend keeping both a file and a copy-and-paste of your contacts in your email accounts and/or in cloud accounts in case something urgent comes up and you have to contact someone. Sometimes, if you have to use a different computer, it may not allow you to open files out of safety, because the server may not recognize it. If you don't want copies of your documents saved on shared computers, copying and pasting your info into an email will enable you to view your info as you normally would, without having to download the info onto a shared computer.

USB sticks can also be used as long as you have them password protected so nobody else can access your info in case you lose them. Using a cloud account is your best option as you don't have to carry anything extra with you; however, it does require you to have an internet connection, which you won't always have in developing countries. In this scenario, a USB stick would be another way to cover yourself.

Emergency contact at home. Give them your itinerary before you leave with all your doctor's info, meds, etc. Keep a copy of all that info in your wallet in case you are in an accident, and the paramedics look through your wallet/purse.

If you need info, head to a fancy hotel. They have phones, bathrooms, money exchange, tourist info, etc. All in one place.

Passport

Make sure you have at least six months left before your passport expires, or immigration agents in most countries won't accept it. You also have to have some empty pages. It's best to order a business passport when you get your passport or renew it. Business passports have more pages for stamps.

While traveling to South Africa, I had a one-day layover in Frankfurt, Germany. After a day of sightseeing, I tried to board the plane to continue my journey. However, the staff wouldn't allow me to board the flight because, according to them, I had several pages in my passport that had one stamp only but none that were completely empty. The South African immigration wouldn't allow me to enter without having a blank page in my passport. I proceeded to the restroom where I used nail polish remover, I had purchased at the airport to remove some of the stamps.

When I went back to try to board the plane, the staff were onto me and didn't allow me to board. I had to spend an extra night in Frankfurt so I could go to the U.S. Consulate in the morning and pay to have them staple and glue additional pages to my passport for a fee of $50. This allowed me to continue on my trip, and after some haggling with the staff, they excused the extra charges resulting from my missing my original flight.

If you lose your passport while traveling, you can go to your embassy or consulate with your digital or paper copies and buy a new passport.

Bills and Financial Information

Just imagine you go on a trip, something changes in your life, and you all of a sudden have a lot of time to burn. You now have three months instead of three weeks to travel.

My boss once did me the favor of notifying me the day before I was scheduled to return to work, after being off for three weeks, that the state had never mailed them proof that my license had been renewed. Apparently, the check I sent to the state board was cashed, but something happened, and my license was not renewed. Therefore, the process would now take three months to complete.

Meanwhile, I would be disallowed from returning to work (unpaid of course) until I received my new license. Well, I wasn't going to let a travel opportunity like this pass me by. But, I had all this mail at home, and I needed to go through it all and pay my bills; otherwise, my credit would be ruined, and my finances would be put into disarray.

As a result, I would recommend that you enroll all your

bills in auto-pay and make all your accounts paperless so you can access your information from anywhere in the world. Same with your paychecks, retirement payments, or pensions. Have them all pay directly into your bank accounts and store the passwords in your two email or cloud accounts. Don't allow bills and mail to dictate your travel schedule.

For other mail, have a friend collect your mail, review, and send you a picture of the contents every couple of weeks. Or you can get a P.O. Box and sign up for USPS Informed Delivery service. Your letters are scanned, and you receive an email summarizing the mail you received.

There are also mail scanning services available such as Traveling Mailbox. They'll open your mail and scan it with your permission, forward it, hold it, and some will also respond to the letters for you as well.

Before every trip, make sure you contact the banks that issued your credit and debit cards and let them know you're on vacation and for how long so they don't block your cards. This has happened to me, and often the banks won't reinstate your cards until you call them from your home phone. Mostly, your card will be useless until you get back home from your trip. It's also best to leave the cash advance option on travel credit cards to zero in case you get robbed.

My brother Bobby had an economist friend who traveled to Mexico City for an economics conference. One night he walked out of his luxury hotel to the sidewalk to grab a taxi, and a VW van pulled up close to him as if they were dropping off someone. Instead, a guy pulled a fabric bag over his head, while two other guys grabbed him and dragged him into the van, and they drove off. He said they forced him to go to an ATM to withdraw the maximum amount allowed from each credit card. After they got all of the money they could get, they took his clothes and left him naked at the side of the road.

A similar incident happened to a chiropractor friend of

mine who traveled with his partner to Mexico City, except the kidnappers demanded my friend's family in Los Angeles to wire ten thousand dollars to a bank account in order to release them from the house where they were being held.

Another thing to keep in mind is what do you do if you can't access any cash. One year during the holidays, I was in Italy, and my cards were all blocked just as I ran out of hard cash. The banks wouldn't bail me out, and the ones that might have, were closed for the holidays. I had to hustle and use what little I had as collateral to get cash from a girl I met at my youth hostel. If you lose your wallet and have no money, head to your local embassy or consulate. They will provide you with temporary travel documents so you can have money wired to you.

Chapter 6.

Travel Communication

The Radio Towers Above the Hollywood Sign, Hollywood California

My friend Justin from Las Vegas recently called me from Burma and said, "Ernesto, my boss wants to speak to me, and he doesn't know I'm in Burma. How do I know when he calls, and how do I call him without getting into trouble?"

Set up your home telephone and cell phone with voicemails and passwords so you can access them remotely. Keep in mind that most people never set up passwords on their cell phones because they've never had to reach their cell phone remotely from a third-party phone.

Set up an autoresponder on your cell phone and email account so that a message is sent to people who are texting or emailing you. A good message would say you're out of the country, out of town, or out of the office, include your email address in the text message, and request that they email you so that you can respond. This will help ensure that you don't miss anything important while you're traveling.

Also, set up a Skype account, LINE, WhatsApp, Google Talk, etc. I use Skype, and it's a penny to call from anywhere in the world to the USA. I also use voice-to-text services such as PhoneTag, that'll send you a text of your voice messages when they come in. You can also set up temporary or long-term secondary phone lines for people to call you using Google Talk or Burner App.

Most cell phone companies have an international plan you can use while traveling. Some even have free data and texting while overseas, although you should confirm to see the average data speeds, cost of WiFi calls, etc. Google Fi wireless is a good option available in most parts of the world and allows you to call in and out of over 200 countries at no extra cost.

Smartphones

Smartphones are possibly the greatest invention ever. I remember reading an issue of Time Magazine that had an article on the greatest invention of the decade and maybe ever: "The Apple iPhone." I agree it's incredible for travel. You can use it to do hundreds of thousands of different things, literally. You can shop around in the App Store for thousands of apps that you may find beneficial for your trip.

Your smartphone can be used to pay your bills, conduct business, to write this book, as a flashlight, maps, GPS, to buy flights, to book hotels, to create PDFs, to e-sign documents, to take pictures, for translation, for scanning, faxing, or for just about everything else.

It saves you from having to haul around a laptop or pay for the use of an Internet café. You can also store information on it as well. Just make sure you install or activate an application for finding your phone if you ever lose it, or so you can wipe it clean remotely in case you can't retrieve it, protecting all of your personal info.

You can even plug it in occasionally and transfer your information, pictures, etc. into your online account as a backup. At airports and venues, you can often show them your digital ticket on your phone to gain entrance to places.

If you're going somewhere you've never been before, use digital travel guides such as Lonely Planet, Frommer's, Barefoot, or Let's Go. These guides are full of everything you'll need for travel, such as maps, where to stay, where to eat, sites to visit, history, customs, etc. They will give you very specific and detailed information on each location you'd like to visit. Therefore, there are hundreds of them, and it's best to get an updated version that has all the latest recommendations for restaurants, activities, and contacts for resources. The difference is that those books are an encyclopedic collection of information, while this book is a general guide book that can be applied to everywhere you go.

Expect to be on boats, planes, trains, and automobiles while on your vacation. Why not sharpen your skills, learn a language, or read those books you've been putting off reading? By downloading them into your phone, you will save space and have fewer items to carry along. Get yourself a library card, and you can check out thousands of books for free with your smartphone to read while you're on your trip. I use an app called Overdrive that allows me to check out eight books at a time for three weeks. You can renew if you need more time. You can also download and pay for subscription services such as Audible, Epic, or Amazon Kindle, which give you more book options or options to buy and own a copy of a digital book.

I recommend an excellent smartphone cover such as an Otter Box, and cell phone battery banks to use in case you can't get a charge. This will last up to a week without charging, depending on your usage. I don't use the covers that have built-in batteries as they drain and damage your phone's battery. They also have waterproof covers in case your iPhone gets exposed to water. Almost all electronic devices now use USB cords, so bring extras with you in case you leave one behind or it gets damaged.

Smartphones also have extra zoom lenses that would be beneficial if you're going on a safari in Africa or trekking in the jungles of South America and need to zoom in on distant wildlife.

Buying a SIM card in the countries you travel to will allow you to use your phone and access messages without the roaming charges. Having access to Google Maps to find walking and driving directions, WhatsApp, Facebook Messenger, Skype to call people, and translation apps to communicate with locals will make things much easier for you. Generally, you can't make international calls unless you have a global calling plan or you'll be charged according to your phone plan.

Laptops

Use Google Drive or GoToMyPC so you can have remote access to your files on your home computer while you're on the road.

For storage in the cloud, Google Drive, Dropbox, and OneDrive are some of the most popular cloud storage companies. These allow you to store everything online and access your files from any computer any time you need something.

If the information you're using on your computer is of vital importance, then invest in cybersecurity suites such as Jungle Disk or Carbonite. This will help prevent your information from being hacked or stolen while you're traveling around and logging into shared networks.

Postal Mail

If you need to send letters, invoices, notices, contracts or other paperwork, you can use Postal Methods to do it for you. You simply email them what you need in a letter, and they'll print it up how you want it, collate it, insert it into an envelope, apply postage, and mail it on your behalf.

For managing postal mail coming to your address, you can use Earth Class Mail to help you. Earth Class Mail allows you to set up a virtual address in most major U.S. cities. Your mail is then routed to their secured facilities. You can use your computer or smartphone to check your mail as PDF documents that are automatically organized for you. Once you review your mail, you can trash and recycle junk mail, deposit checks, download important documents to save, or forward to your attorney, accountant or colleague. Once you're done you can choose to store it, shred it, or recycle it.

Wi-Fi

McDonald's, libraries, Starbucks, malls, and most cafés have free Wi-Fi. More and more public spaces such as parks and transportation areas are also offering free public Wi-Fi around the world.

How to Get Around Limited Internet Access

Most airports, hotels, and other public areas will give you time-restricted wireless internet, so you can then purchase internet service from them. When you log on to a network, it copies your device's media access control (MAC) address, which is a set of letters and numbers that uniquely identify your network card. The MAC address from your tablet, phone, or laptop will then be used for authentication and for the vendor to track your time online. Once you reach your 30 min limit, the system will kick you off the internet and offer you the option to purchase more time online for a set price.

You can get around this by using software to change your MAC address, also known as spoofing. MAC addresses are hard-coded into network interfaces, but free programs like Mac Makeup for Windows and LinkLiar for Mac OS X. These programs change your MAC address so you can keep getting back onto the network with a different address as if you were a new computer.

Step-By-Step MAC Spoofing Using LinkLiar

To d56780-emonstrate how straightforward spoofing +our MAC address is, here's precisely how to do it using LinkLiar for OS X. (Windows users, the process is the same using Mac Makeup.)

1. Download LinkLiar at either CNET's LinkLiar page or GitHub's download page, download the half megabyte application file, and install it.

LinkLiar Mac OS X

2. Open System Preferences, click the purple LinkLiar icon. Follow the prompts to close System Preferences, then reopen it. Click OK. Once System Preferences comes back up, click the LinkLiar icon again.

3. When LinkLiar opens up, it shows your network interfaces with their current MAC addresses shaded in gray. Click your Wi-Fi adapter (this would work for Ethernet connections as well), then toggle the fake MAC address by clicking the little wheel. Hit Apply, then you'll be prompted to type in your administrator password.

LinkLiar OS X

4. Stay in System Preferences; otherwise, you may have to restart the process. In the main System Preferences panel, click Network, which will open up the Networking Preferences window. In this new window, in the left sidebar, click in this order: Wi-Fi > Assist Me > Diagnostics > Continue > Continue > Allow > Quit

5. Clear your browser cache (Firefox, Chrome, Internet Explorer, and Safari) or open a new private browsing window (Incognito in Chrome).

Once you get the hang of it, this entire process takes less than a minute to have access to unlimited free Wi-Fi. You can keep repeating as needed.

Make a note of your true MAC address on OS X and Windows in case your home or office network implements any MAC filtering. There are no adverse side effects of MAC address spoofing. If no free wireless networks are being offered, you can uncover hidden networks using NetStumbler.

Chapter 7.
Food Safety

Traditional Palestinian Meal

Food

The combination of dryness and low pressure inside a plane reduces a person's taste buds' sensitivity to sweet and salty foods by around 30%, leading people to believe that airplane food is not very tasty. Choose the Asian-vegetarian option on the plane. You get your meals before anyone else, and the special-order meals tend to be fresher and have better quality ingredients.

Eating choices while on vacation are going to be determined by your budget and diet regimen. I'm vegetarian, mostly gluten-free, and often on a budget, so I usually carry a few protein bars, meal replacement bars, or nuts (fruit often gets confiscated), so I have something to snack on during domestic travel, saving me money on having to eat low-quality processed food on airlines or in airports. You may even bring a few extras if you're going somewhere expensive like Moscow or Tokyo, so you can have something to snack on during your days. An empty water bottle also comes in handy as you can fill it up at a water fountain and reuse it. It's eco-friendly, and you won't spend money on plastic bottles of water laced with carcinogens like BPA.

Remember, this is where most people's trips get to be affected in a pleasant way (Anthony Bourdain exploring foods) or in a wrong way, getting stuck way out somewhere with a life-threatening sickness or parasites. This is a personal choice that is going to vary depending on your food preferences and how sensitive your body is to certain foods. Generally speaking, it's best to eat vegetarian while you're traveling as meats tend to have a higher risk for foodborne illnesses. Trust your nose, not your eyes. Smells are important indicators of the quality of food.

Be aware of who is handling the food. Avoid establishments where the food handlers don't practice good hygiene, such as tying back their hair, wearing protective gloves, and having clean hands and fingernails. If you see food servers smoking, touching their faces, eating out of pots, chewing gum, sneezing or coughing near food, avoid purchasing food from that vendor.

Look for crowds. When surveying the street food scene in any location, look for groups. Locals get sick too, and won't return to stalls suspected of serving unsafe food; so if there's a crowd, it's usually a safer choice to make. Chances are the food is fresher and cleaner since they are selling it quickly before it has time to sit and grow bacteria or have flies lay eggs in it.

This is how I caught salmonella in Thailand: I ignored the advice of the local Thai people to avoid a certain Indian food restaurant in Chiang Mai. When I walked in, I ordered a large sampler dish. I was so impressed that they had it ready in about three minutes, not thinking that it had already been sitting out in the 100-plus weather. After I finished eating, I ventured up a mountain to my private villa and wasn't able to leave for three days due to diarrhea and vomiting. I slept for about 23 hours and 45 minutes a day. I can only remember opening my eyes for a few minutes and quickly cutting up, aerating, and eating as many cloves of raw garlic as I could until I passed out again. My saving grace was the fact that I had a fresh braid of garlic with me. Garlic is antiviral, antibacterial, antiparasitic, and it's great for supplementing most treatments of travel bugs. In this case, I believe it saved my life! I recommend carrying garlic with you when you're traveling for any intestinal problems. Merely mixing in some into your dishes, will help neutralize some of the adverse effects the food could have on you.

Be selective when choosing foods. Since raw food is subject to contamination, travelers should try to avoid salads, uncooked vegetables, and unpasteurized juices and milk products. Dry foods such as cakes, cookies, and bread are safer options, although not as healthy.

Spice things up. Become familiar with spices such as chilies and turmeric, which are known to have antibacterial properties, and seek out dishes that include them. Acidic fruits, such as citrus fruits and pineapple, are also safer bets when traveling. Because of the higher vitamin C content, they give you an immune system boost.

Avoid over-handled foods such as bulk bin food where people are handling the food items. Avoid foods that require a lot of handling before serving or that contain raw or undercooked meat or seafood. In most cases, meals that are boiled are safer to consume.

Wash vegetables and fruit before eating. If you purchase fresh produce from a roadside stand, be sure to wash and peel them before eating. Bacteria can be present on their exterior and transferred into the edible section once sliced. So make sure you clean the fruit before slicing into it.

If you're traveling in an area with unsafe water, be sure to clean the produce with bottled or filtered water and vegetable cleaner, vinegar, peroxide, or soap.

Eat hot foods hot, and cold foods cold. If the dish you ordered is supposed to be served hot, make sure it is hot when it is served to you. The same is true for any foods that are intended to be served cold. Otherwise, it may not be safe to eat.

Remember the one-hour rule. Don't consume any perishable foods that have been sitting out beyond an hour when the temperature is higher than 90 degrees Fahrenheit.

Wash Your Hands

Before eating or handling food, wash your hands with soap and water for at least twenty seconds. A good rule is to sing the happy birthday song in your head while you wash your hands. Once you're done singing the song, you're done washing your hands. If freshwater is scarce, use antibacterial hand gels or wipes to help keep your hands clean, especially after using the restroom and before eating.

If you have kids, you are elderly, immunocompromised, or get sick often, then sanitize "high touch" areas. Germs linger longer on nonporous materials like plastic. When traveling via plane, train or bus, wipe down common surface areas such as tray tables, seat armrests, and lavatory door handles with alcohol-based wipes or gel before you touch them. If you're staying at a hotel, do the same for the TV remote controls, bathroom door handles, and the telephone.

Don't use antibacterial products that are not alcohol-based; most are made with triclosan. Triclosan causes hormonal irregularities in humans, is toxic for the environment, and causes drug-resistant strains of bacteria.

If you're healthy, then don't bother. The more you are exposed to germs, the stronger your immune system will be. The less you are exposed, the more vulnerable you are, and the more you'll get sick. I generally don't wipe anything down, but I do carry a bar of soap with me to wash my hands whenever I can.

Drink

Boil tap water before consuming. If you need to use tap water from an unknown source, be sure to boil it first for several minutes at a good rolling boil. Also, avoid consuming beverages that may be mixed with the local tap water supply, like juices or sodas from sources such as fountain machines or drinks containing ice, since freezing does not kill most microorganisms.

Beverages made with boiled water and served steaming hot (such as tea and coffee) are generally safe to drink. A friend of mine once got sick from eating butter that had been chilled with ice that was contaminated with microorganisms. It's best to avoid ice.

Not all bottled water is safe. Bottled water products in certain countries can be unclean or even counterfeit (i.e., refilled from a local tap source, which is common in India and China), so always check the seal to ensure it is intact.

In general, be careful with drinks of any kind when going out to a bar or nightclub or just having lunch. This is often the easiest way for people to slip drugs into your drinks and rob you or take advantage of you. I've had many friends go out to clubs, meet someone, and wake up somewhere with all their personal belongings gone. Carry your own water bottle, refill it yourself in reliable places, and if you're going out, open sealed drinking containers yourself. You can also carry iodine tablets and portable water filters with you, so you're not buying plastic bottles and creating more trash.

Tips for Saving on Meals

Food is going to be your third most significant expense after transportation and accommodations. The easiest way to save is to cook it yourself. You can spend as much on eating out in one day as you'd pay for a week's worth of cooking your own meals. If you don't know how to cook, watch some YouTube videos on how to cook beans and rice dishes, they're inexpensive, filling, and healthy. Bring a refillable bottle, so you don't have to keep buying bottled water. Avoid eating in tourist areas, these are by far the most expensive places to eat. Wherever you're staying, ask for recommendations for low-cost local places to eat. Locals will always know the best budget places to eat, wherever you are.

Chapter 8.

Accommodations

Overwater Bungalows in Tahiti.

Where to Stay

Accommodations are going to be your second most significant expense after your airfare. Youth hostels, pensions, and renting rooms from families are my favorite options. Information on all of these is readily available in the travel guides Lonely Planet, Barefoot Guides, Let's Go, Frommer's, etc. Craigslist is my personal favorite because it has the most economical accommodations.

Shared spaces are going to be the lowest priced and offer the best opportunities to meet people. Learning to stay in shared spaces will help you feel comfortable trusting and being open to people you don't know, who are helping you, giving you rides, and in whose houses you are staying. Hostels are the best places to meet other travelers and staff who are knowledgeable about travel.

Once I traveled alone to Chiapas in southern Mexico with the understanding that my brother Bobby would be going with me. Well, as usual, Bobby kept delaying and ultimately ended up not showing up for the trip. Meanwhile, he had booked a room in the most beautiful hotel in town. He urged me to please stay there, because it was already paid for, or it was going to go to waste. I finally agreed and settled in the luxury room with feather down comforters, water fountains everywhere, and staff waiting to do anything I wanted at my request. The only problem was, I was bored and lonely in my luxury room. No one to talk to or exchange ideas with, so I went out to the shared spaces to speak to staff and to look for other travelers to share stories with. There were none, everyone was in his or her room watching cable TV.

After one night, I left and checked into the nearest youth hostel where I made friends quickly with multiple people whom I've stayed in contact with for years; a militant vegan from London, a writer from Puerto Rico, and a shaman from the Lacandon Jungle. These people made my trip exciting, and we joined forces for various excursions and nightlife outings. To date, I have dozens of friends from all over the world, whom I enjoy visiting, hosting, traveling with, and simply sharing my life with. Unfortunately, on this particular trip, I did catch scabies at the hostel. However, those are quickly cured by applying scabicide cream all over the body and not showering for twenty-four hours until the poison has done its thing.

My favorite websites for finding the best accommodation deals.

- HomeAway
- TrustedHousesitters
- Airbnb
- Orbitz
- Booking.com
- Craigslist
- Hostelworld
- Agoda

- Hotels.com
- Couchsurfing
- Priceline.com

Hostels

Hostels, or youth hostels, are my favorite places to stay. Most of the rooms are dormitory-style with shared facilities. Many hostels also offer private rooms like hotels and a lot of the same amenities such as: Wi-Fi, tour services, desks, kitchens, bars, curtains, laundry, lockers for your stuff, big bathrooms, and restaurants.

Hostels offer you an unparalleled opportunity to meet other travelers from all over the world. I've met some of the most exciting people in hostels, as they tend to attract an eclectic bunch. You'll meet people of various ages, interesting backgrounds, and cultures. The staff and fellow travelers are also a valuable resource for travel tips.

Hostel accommodations cost from $2-$50 a night for a dorm bed, and more for private rooms or rooms for fewer people. The best website to find hostels is Hostelworld. Hostels are plentiful, safe, inexpensive, and secure.

Hospitality Exchanges

Hospitality Exchange or Home Stay is a form of accommodation where you are staying as a guest in someone's home for an agreed time and, in turn, you'll be hosting them in your home at another time. It can be free or for a charge, and sometimes it's in exchange for work or services at the host's property.

Hospitality exchanges are a great opportunity to stay with locals and see how they live. These folks are also the most knowledgeable about their surroundings, and they can show you places you'd never be able to find on your own. My hosts have taken me to weddings, birthdays, churches, family, dinners, and several places that you can't find in the guide books.

Hospitality exchanges, help you save on accommodations so you can travel for more extended periods. The best sites are; GlobalFreeloaders, HospitalityClub and CouchSurfing.

My favorite site is CouchSurfing.com because it is well organized, and it has profiles of the hosts you'll be staying with. I recommend reading the hosts' profiles, staying with hosts who have verified accounts, and have a profile picture.

Before you confirm your stay with a host, you should chat with them and make sure your expectations are in line with one another.

Short Term Rentals

Short term rentals are cheaper than hotels and provide many more amenities. They are especially useful if you have pets or a large group because they can come with a kitchen which would save you on food costs. Another great thing about short term rentals is the unique opportunities they offer; I've stayed in a treehouse, igloo, and a teepee.

The best sites are; HomeAway, Wimdu, 9Flats, OneFineStay.com, Booking.com, FlipKey, VacationRentals.com, and Airbnb.

Monasteries

Monasteries offer basic accommodations and often come with a meal included. The locations are run by monks or nuns and usually have a curfew for guests. They often come with a desk, chair, and bed, unless you're staying in the dormitories. Monasteries are family-friendly, in historic buildings, and quiet. Many of the monasteries are free, ask for a donation, or start around $20.

Resources for finding a monastery:

Northeast U.S.

Holy Cross Monastery: West Park, New York. Guests

stay in former monk's quarters, with a bed, dresser, desk, lamp, and shared bathrooms. Meals are eaten with the monks, and the prayer services are open to guests. The recommended donation is $70 per night.

Mount Saviour Monastery: Pine City, New York. The men's section has fifteen small, private rooms; the women and couples' section have two double rooms and three single rooms. Also available are three separate bedrooms, each with a kitchen area. The recommended donation is $40 per night per person.

Society of Saint John the Evangelist: Cambridge, Massachusetts, and West Newbury, Massachusetts. Spiritual retreats are offered. The recommended donation ranges from $60 per night to $95 per night.

Southeast U.S.

Abbey of Gethsemani: New Haven, Kentucky. Guests have been staying here since it opened in 1848. Guests are encouraged to assist the monks during communion, and monks are available for consult. Each guest room has its own shower. Donations are on a free-will basis.

Mepkin Abbey: Moncks Corner, South Carolina. This monastery offers facilities to people for short (1-6 days) retreats and long (30 days) term stays. Visitors observe the same silence as the monks, eat the same vegetarian meals and can take part in the services. The monks of Mepkin Abbey belong to the worldwide Order of Cistercians of the Strict Observance.

St. Bernard Abbey: Cullman, Alabama. Guest rooms for men are air-conditioned with a shared bathroom; women and couples have air-conditioning and a private bathroom. Guests eat with the monks; dinner is a formal monastic meal. Donations are made on a free-will basis.

Midwest U.S.

Monastery of the Holy Cross: Chicago, Illinois.

Individual guest rooms with a shared bathroom. Guests can join the monks in daily services. Monks are available for spiritual assistance. A $25 deposit is requested, but donations are on a free-will basis.

Our Lady's Monastery: Coleman, Michigan. Four guest rooms, all with single beds (six beds are available, you can have four more guests if sleeping bags are used). The monastery is located on the Chippewa Indian reservation in a rural setting. The cost is $40 to $50 daily.

St. Gregory's Abbey: Shawnee, Oklahoma. Weekend retreat dates are posted at this monastery's website. The daily rate is $62 per person. Two individual guest rooms also are available.

St. John's Abbey: Collegeville, Minnesota. Individual and group retreats are available, to accommodate twelve to fifteen people. This is a personal retreat where you will meet with a spiritual director once a day.

West U.S.

Assumption Abbey: Richardton, North Dakota. The monastery started in 1899. They offer retreats as a monastic live-in experience at this monastery.

Incarnation Monastery: Berkeley, California. A few blocks from the University of California at Berkeley campus. All rooms are for single occupancy; each room has a half-bath and a personal garden. The suggested donation is $60 to $70 per night.

Europe

Buckfast Abbey: Devon, England. The only English monastery to be restored and used for its religious purpose after the destruction of monasteries under King Henry VIII. It has been open since 1018.

Home Exchanges

A direct swap of homes between two members, usually

at the same time. Before the exchange you will go through various levels of verification, then you communicate with each other before you make the trade to set up parameters for the transfer. It's an excellent way to live in a new city, have all the comforts of home, and not have to pay any bills. These types of exchanges are beneficial as people tend to be very respectful of one another's homes. You can also have family or friends check up on your guests to make sure everything is going well.

You can get all the comforts of home (hot water, laundry, etc.) while in another city, without paying for it. The best top sites are; iHEN, HomeExchange, Craigslist, and Home for Exchange.

House Sitting

If you don't have a home to swap or would prefer not to do so, then you can trade labor for a place to stay. In exchange for watching someone's house, watering their plants, feeding their pets, and keeping it clean. You get to stay in their homes. This is an excellent option if you're looking for a place to stay for a prolonged period.

The best sites are; Craigslist, MindMyHouse, Luxury House Sitting, and HouseCarers.

Stay on a Farm

You can live on a farm and learn valuable skills through WWOOF-usa. The farms offer educational opportunities like beekeeping, growing veggies, caring for animals, and winemaking. You can either trade labor for free room and board or pay for your accommodations and observe. Similar to a bed and breakfast and rates start at around $40 per night. The best sites; WWOOF-usa, Farm Stay USA, Farm Stay UK, Farm Stay Australia, and Farm Stay Planet.

Hotel Rooms

When booking a room or transportation, be aware of local holidays. This can significantly affect the price, availability, and options when planning your trip. Travel websites often give discounts to people who book flights and rooms together. Block-booked hotel rooms are released at 6 pm, so often you can find good last-minute deals after 6 pm.

If you have a room booked, arriving late can help you get a free room upgrade if all the other rooms booked.

Free Accommodations

Go to a bus station, buy the cheapest bus passage available, pin the ticket to your shirt, and go to sleep on a bench. Having a visible ticket will keep security from bothering you while you rest. When you wake up, you can get a refund for the unused ticket. I used this hack for traveling through Europe and the USA on a minimal budget. This allowed me and my belongings to be safe while I slept for free in bus and train stations.

Chapter 9.

Travel Transportation Secrets

The Pyramids of Giza, Egypt, on a 130* Day.

Transportation varies from country to country, but the usual methods are generally available: cars, buses, trains, planes. Subways operate the same everywhere in the world.

Subways are a fast way to get the layout of a new city. Most subways also offer free maps that you can use to guide you around the city, helping you avoid traffic, and the need to ask for directions. In Europe and most other countries, this is standard practice. However, in North America, it is a skill one must develop as the culture here is more car-oriented.

By using subway stops as reference points, you can

immediately familiarize yourself with a new city. Use these landmarks as points of reference as you look for other locations in the city. This will help you keep track of where you are as you walk around the city.

How to Get In and Out of the Airport Faster Using 3 Hacks

TSA PreCheck

US citizens and permanent residents who travel mostly in the USA can apply for a 5-year TSA PreCheck membership for $85. Children ages twelve and younger may use the TSA PreCheck lane when traveling with a parent or guardian who is a member. Enrollment requires an in-person interview, usually at an airport.

Members receive expedited airport screening through dedicated security lanes and are not required to remove belts, laptops, liquids, or shoes. Most airlines participate except for low-cost carriers.

Global Entry

US citizens, permanent residents, and citizens of select countries who travel internationally can apply for the Global Entry program with a valid passport and a non-refundable $100 application fee. After a background check, an in-person interview will be scheduled. Once you are approved, the membership will be valid for 5 years.

Members receive expedited clearance at Customs and Border Protection checkpoints at most US airports and select international airports.

Travelers can skip long lines and instead scan their fingerprints at automated machines without filling out any forms. Members of Global Entry are automatically eligible for TSA PreCheck.

For anyone planning to travel abroad in the next five years, paying the extra $15 for Global Entry is a no-brainer to get the benefits of both programs.

Generally, you have to make an appointment and wait a few weeks, if not months, for your interview. Additional family members have to apply and interview separately.

Global Entry has two other related programs, NEXUS, and SENTRI, which will assist travelers crossing the Canadian and Mexican borders.

CLEAR

US citizens and permanent residents over eighteen with a valid passport or photo ID can use the CLEAR program to get through security at participating airports with a fingerprint reader. The standard membership for the CLEAR program is $179 per year, additional family members over eighteen can be added for $50, and children under eighteen are free with a CLEAR member, ClearMe.com.

By combining TSA PreCheck and CLEAR memberships, you can conveniently get through the two critical points of security at the airport.

Airplane Tickets: 27 Ways to Save on Flights

Airline tickets typically go on sale eleven months before flight dates, so you can save on tickets to popular destinations and during peak travel times if you buy as far in advance as you can. If you're flexible, then, last-minute travel can give you even better deals. Try using Google Flights, Fly.com, Orbitz, CheapOair, The Flight Deal, Secret Flying, Holiday Pirates, SkyScanner, Hopper, Travelzoo, and many more travel sites' monthly flight fare charts to find the least expensive days to fly in any given month.

If you have to travel during a busy time like Christmas or during school holidays, then definitely book early, because these tickets don't usually go down in price, only up! The best time of the year to score the best prices is usually September and January.

1. Search for plane tickets one at a time even if you're flying with a group. Airlines often sell multiple fare classes

at different prices, with a couple of seats in each category. If there's only one seat left in the lowest fare class and you search for four seats, most automated systems will show you the highest fare class for all four tickets. Try searching one at a time, just in case there are limited seats on sale. This way, you'll rest assured that at least some, if not all, of your tickets, were purchased for the lowest possible price.

If for some reason you don't like your seats, or you don't get all of the seats you want, most websites give you 24 hours to cancel flights with no penalty.

If you lock in the cheap fare and have the option to select seats, pick one next to an empty seat; then, immediately book the second ticket and select the seat next to the first one. It takes a little time and effort but can really pay off.

2. Search for flights midweek. Airlines tend to have lower prices from Tuesday through Thursday, so don't limit your searches to the weekends. Fare sales generally target the next 2-3 months of travel and have a 14-21 day advance purchase requirement.

3. No need to avoid flying on the actual holiday. Changing your departure or return date by one day can lower your ticket price substantially. Sometimes, flying on the actual holiday like Easter, Christmas, and Thanksgiving can get you the lowest fare, since you most likely missed the holiday, but you'll cash in on the savings. The exception is three-day weekends like Labor Day or Memorial Day. Then, everyone is looking to fly on the actual holiday, so that's the best time to try to add an extra vacation day.

4. Search for two one-way fares, even if they are on different airlines. Some airlines charge extra for a one-way fare, but if demand is down, you can sometimes get better prices by buying two one-way tickets to and from your destination.

5. Starting or ending your trip midweek on a Tuesday, Wednesday, or even Saturday, gives you the lowest fares as

these are the days with the least passenger volume.

6. Travel packages are sometimes less expensive. If you need to book a hotel, in some cases packages offer better value than booking separately, since some big-name hotels will use this opportunity to hide their highly discounted rates in package deals to avoid having a discount associated with their name and lower their perceived value.

7. Act quickly on low fares. Airlines are required by the Department of Transportation (DOT) to offer 24-hour free hold on cancellations as long as you are booking your ticket seven days before your travel date. You'll have to pay first, then you get a full refund should you decide to cancel. This applies when buying directly from the airline. However, online travel agencies (OTA), such as Expedia or Orbitz, often offer the same courtesy.

I have booked a few hours before a flight, then hit a snag and was not able to make the flight, so I simply went online and canceled.

8. Use second-tier airports. JetBlue, for example, uses less traveled airports in big cities to lower their ticket prices by $100-$500.

9. Follow your favorite airlines on social media. Use Twitter, Facebook, Instagram, and sign up for travel website emails. This will give you access to deals that airlines can't advertise directly. The fact is that airlines only have a certain number of seats they can advertise at a sale price. Once those are sold the flights go back up to higher tier prices.

10. Sometimes it's better to pay a little more for your ticket when it earns you more points. So you have to compare and see if you gain more from the rewards or the lowest fare. Airline credit cards, as well as travel credit cards, offer free flights for signing up for their services, not to mention perks like priority boarding, free checked luggage, paying your TSA Pre Approved or Global traveler fees, offering insurance, and more.

11. Layovers can be a huge benefit. Even though a nonstop flight is ideal, you can sometimes save hundreds on connecting flights.

Some airlines like Aeromexico, Air France, China Airlines, or Icelandair offer free stopovers. A free stopover is when the airlines offer a night's stay at their connecting hub and you don't get charged for the benefit of staying there. The hub cities are where they concentrate their passenger traffic to save on airline costs. This allows you to save on airfare, visit another city, and make it part of your vacation.

12. In the travel-industry, the calendar year is divided into three seasons: peak season (mid-June through August), shoulder season (April through mid-June and September through October), and off-season (November through March). Shoulder and off-peak seasons are when the travel prices are the lowest. This is when the weather is not ideal and the volume of tourists is lower, or when there is terrible press during political unrest. Destinations will lower their flight and hotel prices to attract tourists to bring revenue into the region, sometimes to half the price or less.

13. If you miss flights often, you can claim back the taxes from your tickets.

14. Travel when the weather is not ideal. For example, the seasons in South America are the opposite of ours. It's winter in the Southern Hemisphere when we have summer; their off-peak season is about May through August. During the off-season, hotels, airlines, and tours are much cheaper.

15. Travel after a natural disaster, a terrorist attack, political violence, or after some other tragic incident occurred. That can get you better deals since people will be canceling their trips and being wary of going to an area under such circumstances. Before you go, make sure to check in on the situation, and wait just enough time till things stabilize. However, there is a short window of opportunity to benefit from the upside of the situation, as

humanitarian aid or security forces rush in immediately afterward, and the area becomes safer than it will probably ever be again.

16. Travel websites often give discounts to people who book flights and rooms together.

17. Fridays and Saturdays are the most expensive time to book hotels and flights, while midweek tends to be the lowest priced. If you have to stay somewhere during that time, stay in a business area. The rooms will be cheaper at that time since people are not conducting business on weekends.

18. Request a seat in the exit row. These seats have the most legroom and are assigned on a first-come, first-served basis.

19. For a free upgrade, wait till the plane is full. Then, ask or wait and give up your seat to people who want to sit together.

20. If your flight is canceled, call the airline or travel agent instead of waiting in line with everyone else; it's faster, and you won't have to compete with the others. You can also ask that your ticket be endorsed to a competing airline.

21. If you have extra carry-on bags and you want to avoid being charged for them, be the last one to board the plane. The staff will be on a time crunch to get everyone boarded and close the gate, or risk making the plane late for departure. This will help you avoid being hassled about your bags or being charged extra baggage fees.

22. Another way to get a free carry-on is to wear a fanny pack and fill it with carry-on items that would otherwise go into your backpack. Fanny packs are free because they are attached to your waist like a belt, where a purse is considered a carry-on bag.

23. If the airline charges for water, a glass of ice is

usually free, so you can order ice and wait for it to melt, or fill it up for free with water in the bathroom at the airport or on the plane, if it's potable.

24. If you're planning to take a long trip, consider the convenience of an around the world ticket. You'll get a bulk price for prebooking several flights at once. Specialized agencies are more knowledgeable, better equipped, and know how to deal with different airlines and connect unusual destinations.

However, if you prefer planning the trip yourself, it's sometimes less expensive to book multiple segments on your own than to buy one around the world ticket and be charged higher fees. Around the world tickets usually cost you more than if you just book the trips yourself. Try comparing both options to see which is more cost-effective and gives you the options you're looking for.

25. **Keep Your Travel Searches Secret**

The cookies in your browser are watching what you search for online. Therefore, when it sees you searching the same routes multiple times, your price will increase. The search website will try to scare you into booking the flight quickly before prices get even higher. You can bypass this by searching for flights in Incognito or private browsing mode to see the lowest prices.

In Firefox or Internet Explorer, hit Command (or Control if using a PC), Shift, "P". In Google Chrome or Safari, Incognito is enabled by hitting Command (or Control if using PC), Shift, "N". This will open a new browser window where your information is not tracked, and preventing the price from going up artificially as you search.

Every time you reopen an Incognito window, your cookies will be reset. So, for every flight search, you want to close all Incognito windows and open a new one. This will prevent the site from remembering your previous searches and inflating your flight costs.

26. Looking for tickets early mornings gets you better prices on flights, because people typically shop for trips in the evenings when they get off from work. As people book flights, the prices go up as the supply of seats decreases. The following day, people may have buyer's remorse; they change plans or they find better prices, and they cancel their flights to be able to get a free refund within the first 24 hours causing the supply of seats to increase every morning, which affects the algorithms that adjust the flight prices. You can see this scenario play out every day as flight prices increase during lunchtime (when people have time to shop for flights), then increase more at night (when people are off from work), and then drop the following morning (as people wake up and cancel trips before they start their day in fear that they might forget and get stuck with a ticket they don't want).

27. Don't jump at the first price you see. If you have luggage, it's better to avoid budget airlines. For example, I bought a round trip flight from Los Angeles to Miami on United or Delta airlines: $305 for the flight and $60 for baggage (one free carry-on and $30 each way for one checked bag,), $365 total ticket price. On Spirit airlines, a roundtrip ticket was only $260, but the baggage fees were $260 ($65 for one carry-on and $65 each way for one checked bag), $520 total ticket price. So, to save $35 on the plane tickets, I would have had to pay $200 extra for my baggage.

Seven Tips on What to Do if You Miss Your Flight

If you miss your flight because the airline overbooked it, then the airline is responsible for booking you on the next available flight and providing you with accommodations and meals if that flight isn't until the following day. If you miss a connection due to an airline's delays (mechanical problems), then the airline should re-book you on the next available flight and, if necessary, provide accommodations and food.

If you miss your flight due to personal reasons (tardiness, flat tire, a family emergency, or health problems), then it's your responsibility.

1. Contact the airline: as soon as you know you're not going to make it or you've already missed the flight contact the airline. If you're at the airport, speak to the gate agent or the ticketing representative. When communicating with agents, be very polite. They decide how they want to handle your ticket, so you want to remain on their good side. Explain your unfortunate circumstance and ask them what options are available. If you have membership status with the airline, mention that to the agents, and they may be more willing to help.

If you're not at the airport, call your airline's local number. Calling the local number will allow you to connect to a gate agent or ticketing representative faster, than if you called the airline's general number. You may be required to pay a ticket change fee and the difference in price if the plane ticket has gone up since you purchased your original ticket, but calling ahead will probably save you from losing the value of the entire ticket.

2. The flat tire rule: when the factors that caused you to miss your flight are totally out of your control, some airlines have (unwritten) rules that may make them a little more lenient in the face of your predicament. If you arrive at the airport within two hours of your missed flight, and you have a good excuse for being late, they may be willing to waive change fees and other additional charges. Politely ask that the "flat tire rule" be invoked.

I have used the flat tire rule several times, and it has been effective every time I've used it. I once wasn't allowed to board a plane because my passport was seven months from expiring, and my trip was for eight weeks, meaning my passport would only be good for five months when I returned from my trip, and airlines do not allow you to travel with a passport that has six months or less before it expires. The agents rebooked my flights at no cost to let me get a new passport.

On another occasion, I was on a two-day layover in

Europe on my way to Africa. When I tried to check-in for the second leg of the flight, the agent checking me in would not allow me to board because the country I was traveling to would not allow me to enter without having two empty pages in my passport, one for the entry and one for the exit.

3. Blanket waivers: Whenever there's a significant regional flight disruption, due to weather or other factors, airlines will issue blanket waivers allowing all passengers to change their flights for any reason at no charge. You might be able to use one of these waivers if you're running late.

4. Don't book a new one-way ticket. Sometimes buying one half of the flight is cheaper than paying for the change to your original roundtrip ticket. But in many cases, buying a new one-way ticket cancels the rest of your original itinerary. So, you wouldn't be able to use the second half of your original flight. Check with your airline to confirm which option would be better.

5. Keep connecting flights in mind. If missing your first flight will cause you to lose a connection, notify the gate agent or phone operator so they can help you plan accordingly. If you made the first flight but missed the connecting flight, then most airlines will make you a standby on the next available flight. In this situation, you must call ahead to the airline and baggage claim so they can store any checked bags until you're able to pick them up.

6. Adjust your hotel reservations accordingly. If missing your flight will also cause you to lose a hotel reservation, then notify the hotel as early as possible.

7. In the ever-evolving world of travel, flexibility often equates to money saved. For instance, if you find yourself with a ticket purchased less than 24 hours before your scheduled flight and realize you'll miss it, don't panic. Most airlines, in compliance with federal regulations, allow passengers to cancel their reservation within 24 hours of booking, provided the reservation was made at least a week prior to the departure date. This can be a lifesaver in those

tight spots. I recall a tale of my friend, John, who took advantage of this policy. He booked a flight mere hours before its departure and could not make it due to unforeseen circumstances. Ten minutes before take-off, he quickly called the airline and secured a full refund, all because his plane was still on the tarmac.

However, it's worth noting a significant caveat regarding early check-ins. While they can offer a hassle-free airport experience, enabling travelers to bypass the ticket counter and head straight to security, they might inadvertently bind you to that flight. Once you've checked in, primarily via an airline application, making changes to your reservation or even canceling it without incurring penalties becomes significantly more complicated. So, if you're sure about your travel plans, it might be prudent to hold off on the early check-in until you're at the airport. Doing so keeps your options open and sidesteps potential fees for in-person check-ins, printing boarding passes, or unexpected baggage charges. The key is to strike a balance between convenience and flexibility.

8. If you purchased travel insurance, check your policy stipulations. Some insurance companies will allow you to recoup some or all of your expenses that arise from missing a flight. Read your policy stipulations and figure out what information your insurance is going to require for you to get a refund.

Examples of Some Airline Policies

American has a late arrival standby policy that allows passengers who present themselves at the airport within two hours of departure to be accommodated as a standby flyer on the next flight without paying change fees or fare increases. As long as the scheduled flight is not the last of the day.

Delta has a flat tire rule that applies when "a customer who in good faith arrives late at the airport due to an unforeseen delay." In these cases, customers rely on the discretion of the agents at the airport.

73

Southwest's internal flat tire rule requires passengers to call the airline within 10 minutes of departure if they won't make the flight to retain the flight's cost as a credit. If you're running behind, be sure to arrive at the airport within two hours of the flight's departure. Even if it's the last flight of the day, Southwest will try to accommodate the passenger as standby on the next flight, even if it's the first flight out in the morning.

United requires passengers to present themselves at the airport within two hours of departure.

If you do end up missing a flight, keep things in perspective. Worse things could happen to you, and at least you'll have more time to explore wherever you are. After missing several flights in my life, I've had to pay fees to rebook my trips, but the airlines have always been flexible with me on my particular situations.

Freighter Travel

This is around $139 per day, which includes room, meals, and transportation. Container ships allow limited space for SLF (self-loading freight). Meals are shared with the crew, and the food is usually simple; otherwise, you are left to care for yourself. The ports are generally not close to the most desirable locations, so you'll have to make your own arrangements to go sightseeing.

Some of the ports you visit on freight ships don't have access by plane. The Pacific is one of the best areas to travel by freighter. There is an awesome trip you can take to the Marquesas Islands in French Polynesia for two weeks. On cruise ships, it would cost tens of thousands of dollars to see these islands. These particular trips can be booked up to the day of departure.

Other Pacific cruises can be booked up to a year in advance. Check out The Cruise People. For freight travel to New Zealand, Australia, and the Pacific, check FreighterTravel.co.nz.

Trains

It used to take six months to get from the Midwest to California by wagon train, and one out of every ten passengers died on the way. Once the transcontinental railroad was completed, a person could travel from New York to California in comfort and safety in less than a week.

Trains are one of the most comfortable and environmentally friendly ways to travel. They are much safer and more comfortable than a car or a bus, and you get to see natural environments. Wherever there is a road, there is environmental degradation. Trains, on the other hand, take the path of least resistance through mountains and areas that would not be safe for a car or a bus. Therefore, these spaces tend to have the best scenery and have the best-preserved natural landscape. Trains offer you a continually changing environment outside your window with time to sit back and enjoy the view, or create your own activities.

When you drive long distances on a highway, you're sure to see billboards and businesses catering to the needs of drivers. When you're on a train, you'll see neither as the trains are self-contained and there aren't enough travelers to warrant the marketing investment on these routes.

Flying is convenient for crossing steep terrain faster, but it creates a lot of pollution, and you'll miss out on all the sights below. A train is much slower, but you're going to have an authentic experience. Keep in mind that a train is part of the travel experience, while a plane is the fastest way to get somewhere.

Trains offer two types of travel, coach (seat) or sleeping car (includes a seat that converts to a bed). Some trains also offer business and first-class options with more luxuries. It's best to plan out train trips in advance as seats do fill up, especially sleeper cars, and even more during the summer. Amtrak offers rail vacation packages that save on combinations that include train fare, hotel, and tours.

If you book a trip in coach, pack a blanket and an inflatable pillow, because the train cars are air-conditioned. Neither are provided. Although the items may be for sale on trains, they may be expensive or not always available.

Some trains allow bicycle storage for an extra fee. Check with the train company ahead of time, as some trains only allow bikes on local trains.

Seats in the middle of the train as well as on the second floor will be quieter, smoother, and have the best view.

If you book a trip and there are no sleepers available, there are still two ways you can get a sleeper car last minute. The first is to board the train and immediately ask the conductor if there are any vacancies available. If someone did not make their reservation, you could buy the available sleeper car vacancy. The second is to call Amtrak 1-800-USA-RAIL at 3:30 am Eastern Time and ask for vacancies. At 3:15 am computers erase all of the reservations that people have made and not confirmed. This opens up seats in every category and will give you the first opportunity to buy them as they become available.

Another option is to combine a plane and a train trip on the same journey. For example, you could fly to New York from Los Angeles and ride the train back to Los Angeles. This would save you some time, but still, allow you to see the entire train route.

Individual ticket prices vary according to how flexible you want the ticket to be. The further in advance you buy your ticket, and the more rigid the time frame, the lower the cost. Typically, when you buy tickets on short notice and with fixed travel dates, it's going to cost you more.

Rail passes in Europe, the USA, and elsewhere are more economical, and give you more flexibility. You can buy a rail pass that comes with multiple trips to be used within a set amount of time in a predetermined region. For example, in the USA Amtrak sells passes as indicated below;

Amtrak Passes	California Pass 21 Days, 7 Segments	National Pass 15 Days, 8 Segments	National Pass 30 Days, 12 Segments	National Pass 45 Days, 18 Segments
Adult 16+	$159.00	$459.00	$689.00	$899.00
Youth 13-15		$459.00	$689.00	$899.00
Child 2-12	$79.50	$229.50	$344.50	$449.50

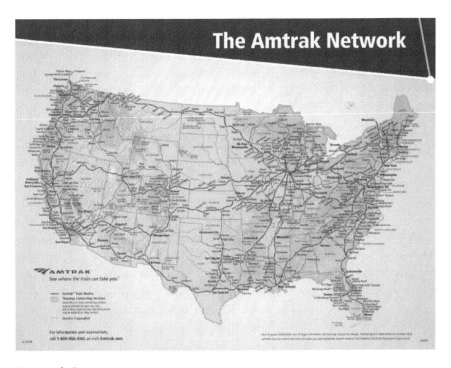

The Amtrak Network

Rental Cars

If you're flying somewhere or taking a train and the local transportation will only get you so far, consider renting a car to increase your possibilities. Renting a car will allow you to plan your own trip, bypass things you don't like, and spend more time soaking in experiences that you're enjoying. Rental cars are a good option for hard-to-get-to places and to save wear and tear on your own vehicle.

Rental cars can be more cost-effective if you're traveling in a group or traveling in a country with limited travel options.

If the car you rent sustains some damage and you have the time, take it to be repaired before you return it. While on a trip through Central America, I lost the hubcaps of my car, so I decided to do a test. I replaced three of them for $10 each and left one missing to see how much the agency would charge me; they charged me $60 for that one.

I was looking up African Safaris in Kruger National Park, South Africa, and the best price I could find was $1,200 per person for six days. I rented a car for $25 a day ($150 for six days), paid $25 a day per person for the entrance fee, less than $5 a day per person on food, $30 for one tank of gas, $50 a night ($300 for 6 nights) for a cabin, and we drove into the park ourselves. There were three of us on the trip, so we would have spent $3,600 for six days of travel, instead we paid $1020 for all of us or $340 each. On this trip, we traveled through twelve countries on our own, which saved us over $35,000 in six weeks off the lowest priced tours we could find.

In some cases, the more difficult the travel challenge, the more rewarding it is to achieve. Driving and hitchhiking to Cancún was a crazy life experience; flying there would have just been a 'trip.'

Thirteen Tips for Renting a Car

1. Take advantage of free car insurance coverage by your credit card company. During a trip to Africa, my rental car was damaged due to break-ins. Luckily, I booked the car with my Visa credit card, so I knew I was covered, but I wanted to get an idea as to how much the repairs would

cost. I took the car to a shop for a written estimate, and I was quoted $1,600. When I returned the vehicle to the car rental agency, they billed me the dealer price of $6,500. After paying a $200 deductible, my Visa insurance reimbursed me the $6,500. Nonetheless, keep this in mind; if your car sustains minor damage under the deductible amount, then go to a local mechanic shop and have it fixed, or use the following strategy in case you didn't use a credit card to book the car.

If you rent a car with a valid Visa card, you will have coverage for covered damage to the rental vehicle for up to 31 days outside of your home country and 15 days inside your country. MasterCard offers similar insurance, but only covers you for 15 days regardless of where you are. For the coverage to be applicable, the cardholder must decline the collision damage waiver (CDW) or similar coverage offered by the auto rental company. The amount of coverage and deductible vary according to your credit card.

2. As soon as you receive your rental car, don't drive away immediately. You don't want to get charged for pre-existing damage to a vehicle. Pre-existing damage to a vehicle is the most common way people get ripped off when renting a car. Take time to inspect the car and let the agent know of any damage before you sign any paperwork. First, take a video and pictures of the car, including its damage and the gas gauge. Take 360-degree photos of the vehicle using a free application like Record360 to document the condition of the car when you pick it up. Don't forget to bend down and get anything that might not be at eye level. Repeat this process when you return the car so that you have a record that no damage occurred while you had the car. Save your images or video for a few months after the rental to make sure you're in the clear. Keeping records will help protect you in case the rental company tries to blame you for damages you didn't cause.

While in Guadalajara, Mexico, I tried to return a rental car that I didn't damage. When I picked up the car, it had several dents, and the agent said those had already been accounted for and not to worry (make sure you get it in writing and take pictures, if this is the case). When I returned the car, another agent was working, and he insisted I was responsible for the damage. Because I had a flight to catch, I wasn't able to stay arguing with him, so I signed "Under Duress" as my signature without telling the agent what I was signing. Don't miss your flight because you're there arguing over fees. Had I not signed, he would not have given me the paperwork stating that I had returned the car, and they would have continued to charge me as if I had not returned it. Do not sign your legal signature, or you'll be legally bound to the terms of the agreement. Once I returned home, I disputed the charge with my credit card company and was successful.

3. Book your car ahead of time. It's highly unlikely that you'll get the best price by just showing up at the rental car counter. Do keep an eye on your car rental prices as prices vary depending on demand, and if there's a price drop, you can cancel your reservation and rent at a lower price.

4. Don't prepay for gas as the car rental companies typically charge above-market rates for gas. Just fill-up the tank within 10 miles of your return location.

5. Ask for a grace period when you check out the car. The agent will typically give you two hours free grace period. If you ask for it at the end of your trip, the car rental companies are reluctant to provide it without charging a late fee.

6. Most companies charge a one-way drop fee, but they may waive it if you ask them to do so before your trip starts.

7. Rental cars at airports are generally more expensive, so find another car rental agency, unless it's too far, that may be cheaper.

8. Pay your toll charges. Renting an optional toll transponder will cost about $5 per day for the duration of the car rental.

9. Decline outdated GPS systems, which usually require $6 to $16 a day for the optional rental. Use your iPhone or Google maps instead.

10. Read the small print in your contract, and don't leave the counter before reviewing your receipt for optional fees. Once you sign and walk away, it'll be difficult to get such charges removed.

11. Shop the travel websites like Orbitz or use your Costco membership to find the best deals.

12. Become an associate member of the American Association of Retired Persons (AARP), which allows you to get savings on car rentals hotels and flights. The annual membership is only $16, and members can join before they meet the age requirements.

13. Consider some of the smaller car companies that sometimes have better rates.

Cruise Ships

- Cruise ship prices are the same on every website.
- Repositioning cruises typically give you the best deals. A repositioning cruise starts and ends in a different port. Cruise ships will relocate to different ports as the season changes or for economic reasons. Fares maybe half the cost of a typical cruise which allows the cruise company to offset the cost of moving their ships to regions where the weather is favorable or there is a higher demand for their tours.
- It's cheaper to cruise when kids are back in school.
- Buy cruise gift cards at a supermarket to get the highest amount of rewards, then pay off your cruise with those gift cards.
- To avoid long lines, pay your cruise account late at night or early in the morning.
- If you're booking a flight to catch your cruise, arrive the day before for the best airfare.
- Baggage limitations are the same as for planes and trains, two bags per person with a 50 lb. limit. As

long as you're reasonable, there are no constraints on liquids.

- Avoid parking at the port, which is usually the most expensive parking. At least one of the nearby hotels or parking lots will have discounted rates for cruisers.
- Avoid boarding early, or you'll have to wait in more lines and for extended periods of time.
- When you arrive on a cruise, ask how much for an upgrade. Sometimes you can get a good deal if some of the better rooms haven't sold.
- Turn your phone on airplane mode on the ship, or you'll get charged high roaming charges.
- Interior cabins are usually the lowest priced.
- For people who get seasick: Cabins in the lower and middle of the ship have less movement.
- Larger cruise ships will offer private in-room babysitting while you go out to party.
- Casino payouts on cruise ships are the worst of any casinos anywhere. However, the poker tables are full of rookies, so if you're a poker player, it's a great place to clean up.
- Most of the stuff for sale in the cruise ship stores go on sale at the end of the cruise.
- Keep yourself extra clean on a cruise ship, and practice good hand hygiene to prevent getting and spreading norovirus which spreads easily.
- Large ships have a morgue in case someone dies.
- Cruise ships do have their own jails in case someone gets out of line.
- Just like on airlines, they check passenger lists and arrest you when you arrive back in port if you're wanted by the authorities.
- When you arrive in port, walk a few blocks to avoid the highest priced transportation.

Hitchhiking

Hitchhiking is an excellent way to learn about cultures and to get to know locals.

One of my first significant trips by myself was during my summer college break when I was twenty-one years old. The university had just let out for the summer, and I wanted to travel.

The first thing I did was ask all my friends if they wanted to take a trip for the summer. Everyone had the usual reasons why he or she couldn't go: "No money, no time, I don't know how to do it, I'm scared, I don't want to leave my girl/boyfriend" etc. I thought about it and asked myself: "Do I want to stay home all summer, or do I want to go see the world?"

The first trip is the scariest. It's like going to the movies by yourself. You feel as if people are watching you everywhere you go.

I started by shopping around the Internet and decided to buy a one-way ticket to Mazatlán, Mexico. I speak Spanish, and I'm familiar with the culture, so this seemed like the right place for me to take my first solo trip. I ended up hitchhiking for three months. I went down to Belize, and then I made my way back up to the state of Chihuahua by the US border. Hitchhiking is a subculture of sharing.

Preparing to Hitchhike: 8 Steps

1. Invest in a good map. A detailed map such as a AAA map is worth the money. As AAA puts it, GPS signals get lost, and phones die, but paper maps are forever reliable. If you need a free map, however, find a tourist spot, such as a hotel, airport, bus station, AAA location for members, or a tourist information booth, and pick up a pamphlet that has a decent map inside. State welcome centers on interstate highways also have free highway maps for their state. Rental car places tend to have the best free maps.

Look for a map that shows road numbers, rest areas, and gas stations. Having a good map will also make you look more knowledgeable and prepared, and thus appealing to drivers. That said, if you have data with a smartphone, that is the ideal way to search and use the most up-to-date maps.

2. Know how to find the right hitchhiking spot. A good place might be near an on-ramp. These locations often have steady traffic and enough space for a car to pull over and pick you up. Stop signs and stoplights are also good choices because it gives drivers enough time to check you out from a distance as they approach and decide whether they want to offer you a ride.

Make sure that you're on the side of the city or town that's in the direction you're traveling. For example, if you're heading west, get on the west side of town. Choose a straight stretch of road so drivers can see you from a distance, an incline would be even better. Choose a place where cars are passing at low speeds, so it's easier for them to stop and pick you up. Make sure that the spot is well-lit. This will not only keep you safe, but also make you more noticeable.

3. Pack as light as possible, but bring enough supplies to last you for a few days. The less you carry, the easier it will be for you to hitchhike and for drivers to want to pick you up. People are more willing to pick you up when they are not inconvenienced. When they stop, you want to get in and out as quickly as possible.

Avoid suitcases and trash bags, as they make you look like you're a vagrant and more of a danger in most people's minds. Use a backpack instead, and you'll look more professional. It's easier to get in and out of cars with a backpack. Pack as though you were going for a three-day hike in case you get stranded and are unable to find a ride.

Consider bringing the following: water, snacks, sunblock, insect repellent, sleeping bag, tent, clothes, light jacket, raincoat/poncho, extra socks, long underwear, a hat, boots, cell phone chargers, and any other care necessities. Don't bring a guitar and/or items of sentimental value as they will simply weigh you down. Consider packing some pepper spray, especially if you are female. Keep in mind that pepper spray is not legal in some areas.

4. Signs are an excellent way to catch people's attention. It lets them know where you're headed and prevents them from making additional stops if they're going in a different direction. It also shows people that you have a plan or destination in mind and you're not just drifting around. Using a bold black marker, write a short message with big letters on a piece of cardboard. This will make your sign easier and faster to read. You can also write the name of your destination to let people know where you're headed. Writing catchy phrases on your sign will also help, such as "Have a nice day" or "God bless" etc.

5. Be aware of the laws. Laws regarding hitchhiking will vary from place to place. For example, hitchhiking is legal in all fifty states of the USA, but how you do it will vary from state to state. In general, however, you should stay off the highways.

6. Make digital copies of all your IDs, documents, and papers. Scan your ID (and passport, if traveling internationally) and email it to yourself. This way, if it gets stolen, print out copies at a library. For passports, go to an embassy or consulate with your copies and do what you need to do to get a new passport. If you lose your credit card, call them immediately, cancel your card, and have them send a new one to an address where you can receive it, like an embassy or consulate.

7. Be prepared financially. Have some backup money, as well as traveler's health insurance. Accidents happen, and you will need to be ready; traveler's health insurance will help you with that. Also, having spare money will help you get food and shelter in the event you are stranded somewhere for longer than you expected.

8. Be mindful of the weather. In most cases, it's better to wait out the rain or snow as drivers are reluctant to pick up drivers who will dampen their seats. Rain will not increase your chances of getting picked up. Snow, however, tends to increase your chances of getting picked up for a ride. If you

carry an umbrella or a raincoat, that will help reassure drivers that you're not going to damage their car.

Safety During Hitchhiking: 7 Steps

1. Be selective about which rides you accept. You'll actually get to your destination faster that way. It's better to travel fifty miles and get dropped off at a gas station or truck stop than to travel a hundred miles and get dropped off in the wrong location for hitchhiking. If you're on a busy roadway for more than two hours and people aren't stopping, you're probably on the wrong road or the wrong side.

Never take rides from anyone who appears intoxicated. This can obviously be dangerous, and if the person gets into a car accident, it can put you in a precarious situation. Don't be afraid to ask the driver questions to get to know them better. Ask them where they are going and why. This might give you a better idea of their intentions.

2. Know that you don't have to accept every car that pulls over. Even if you're desperate, your safety is more important. If you're getting bad vibes from the first car that pulls over after waiting for hours, don't get in. It's not worth the risk. Wait for another car. You should watch out for the following:

Cars that look and/or smell dirty, which implies that the person is not responsible and doesn't care about themselves and quite possibly not for others. Stay out of cars that have bottles of alcohol or beer cans in view; the driver might be intoxicated. Avoid vehicles that have multiple passengers. This means that more people can take advantage of you. Be wary of drivers who give too much or not enough eye contact, because they're usually hiding something. Drivers who are angry, controlling, or impatient may not make your ride enjoyable, but may also not be safe drivers.

Once while traveling in South Africa with my friend Emilio, he accepted a ride from a fellow youth hostel resident so that he didn't have to drive alone to a mutually agreed on location four hours away. Instead, the guy ended up driving seven hours in another direction and was planning to keep my friend with him for weeks because he didn't want to travel alone. Long story short, he dropped off my friend in a random city. The only reason he agreed to drop my friend off was that I told him to tell the guy he had left his wallet in my car.

3. Trust your instincts, and don't be afraid to excuse yourself. If someone pulls over for you and you don't feel safe, you should not hesitate to stand firm and refuse the ride. Or, if you're already in the car and no longer feel safe, politely ask to be let out at the next stop. If that doesn't work, here are some things you could say to excuse yourself: "I'm sorry, I was hoping for a ride that's going farther than that." "Oh no, I think I forgot something back in town. I need to go back. Thank you for the offer." "Ugh... I feel dizzy..." Be sure to look nauseated while doing this. "Oh, I'm sick." People don't like you to throw up in their car.

4. Stay connected to your friends and family. Before going hitchhiking, tell your friends and family where you're going, for how long you'll be gone, and when to expect you back. This way, if something goes wrong and you're gone for longer than expected, they'll notify the police and send someone to look for you. Before you get into a car, it would be a good idea to text the license plate number to a friend. This may help police find you if you do go missing.

Once you're in the car, send friends a text message or call them and let them know where you are. This way, if the driver has evil intentions, he'll be less likely to carry them out.

5. Avoid hitchhiking at night. Not only are the roads more dangerous, but you'll be harder to see. You'll be more likely to get hit by a car than picked up by one. Also, people tend to commit more crimes at night because the darkness gives them cover. Find a place to camp or stay in a motel.

6. Keep your backpack with you at all times. Avoid putting it into the trunk. If you put it there, the driver might drive away with it when he or she lets you off. You will be stuck without supplies for a long time. Keep valuables, such as wallets and phones, on your person at all times. This way, if your bag does get lost, you will still have money and some form of communication on you.

7. Consider bringing a friend if this is your first time. It is always safer to travel in pairs, especially if you are female. It might also be a good idea to hitchhike with a friend who has done this before. You'll feel more at ease, and you'll be less likely to make mistakes. A friend may also help ease boredom and frustration. However, traveling in pairs can make it harder to get picked up.

Presenting Yourself and Practicing Good Etiquette for Hitchhiking: 7 Tips

1. Smile and be approachable. Waiting for a car to stop can take a while, so you might want to do something that will keep you happy, such as singing or listening to music. Avoid sitting or reading a book, as this will make you look bored or unapproachable; it will also take your attention off the road and potential rides. You should also avoid smoking, drinking, or doing drugs. Not all drivers are open to these sorts of activities, and you'll reduce your chances of getting picked up. If someone shouts something rude at you or makes a rude gesture, don't fight back. Simply smile, and let it go. If you start feeling irritable, take a 15 to 20-minute break in a café, or take a nap. Drivers won't pick up someone who looks irritable.

Doing something fun while you wait, such as playing an instrument (something small and easy to carry, like a harmonica), juggling, or dancing, will help make you look more visible and thus appealing. You'll be more likely to pick up a ride. Don't cross your arms or keep your hands in your pockets. You'll look bored and unapproachable. Instead, smile wave, and say hello.

2. Look clean and presentable. This goes for both your

clothes and body. If you look dirty and unkempt, people might mistake you for a homeless person or an escaped prisoner rather than a traveler. People usually don't give rides to homeless people or escaped prisoners. Make sure your hair is brushed and that you're clean-shaven. Make sure that your clothes are neat and clean and not torn or wrinkled.

3. Consider dressing like a local. People tend to warm up to those who dress as they do. This is an important strategy to consider when you are traveling through an area that could be dangerous, where you don't want to be noticed. Consider wearing jeans and a flannel shirt if you are in a working-class neighborhood, and khakis and a collared shirt if you are in a white-collar area.

4. Know what types of clothing to avoid. In general, you should avoid wearing clothing that's dirty, torn, faded, or rumpled. You should also avoid wearing sunglasses, because they'll prevent eye contact and imply that you are hiding something. Avoid wearing black, as it'll make you look more intimidating and harder to see. Opt for lighter or brighter colors. You'll be more visible and more approachable.

Super short hair is often associated with prisons and asylums. People may think that you're on the run from the authorities, especially if the rest of your appearance is ragged. Avoid having long hair and/or a beard as these are often associated with untidiness.

5. Be mindful and respectful of other hitchhikers. If there are other hitchhikers, try to make conversation with them. If they are going in the same direction you are, ask to pair up. It's always safer to travel in numbers. If they're not going in the same direction, then step aside and wait your turn. You can learn a lot from your fellow hitchhikers. They can give you tips on traveling and the surrounding area.

6. Be friendly once in the car. You will likely be in the car for a while, and you don't want the ride to be awkward. Many drivers won't mind talking, and some may even start

a conversation with you by asking about your trip, where you are going, etc. Don't be afraid to ask some questions yourself. Keep personal details to a minimum, at least until both you and the driver feel comfortable. If you're traveling in a foreign country, consider learning some words in their language. Many drivers will pick up hitchhikers out of the need for companionship. Knowing the language will help you carry a conversation. A friendly conversation can also earn you a free meal, an extra mile or two, or helpful information. Never ask for free food, however, but accept it when it is offered. Use your intuition! Avoid sensitive subjects, such as politics, race, and religion. They can make friendly conversations turn unfriendly quickly.

7. Plan ahead for getting dropped off. It would be a good idea to discuss your drop-off location towards the beginning of the ride. Ask to be dropped off at a safe, well-lit area, such as a gas station. Also, ask to be dropped off right before or right after a city; hitchhiking in cities is difficult. Truck stops are great drop-off places. You'll be able to get more supplies and find more rides there.

Road Trips

With road trips, you have two options: plan out a trip or just go. If you're planning a trip, then you'll need reservations for hotels, restaurants (if necessary), and places you'd like to visit while driving. You'll need to calculate the distances and hours that you'd like to drive each day, so you don't run out of time, arrive too early or too late to places. This takes practice, and if you're off by too much, then you'll end up not making reservations, rushing through places, or getting there too late.

Your second option is to figure out generally where you want to go and just go! This can be exciting, and it gives you the flexibility to stay as long as you want in places and change course as ideas come up or your time allows. You'll have to be nimble and book hotels as needed, when you have a better idea of where you'd like to stay. But in the end, it's not much more effort than pre-booking, and you'll avoid all the stress related to having to meet timelines. It also allows you to change course if you find something along the way that catches your interest and that you prefer to invest your time in seeing instead.

If you're driving a recreational vehicle (RV), more planning is recommended as campsites are limited and fill up even during mid-week. RV campgrounds vary from budget state park sites in pristine locations with essential amenities to private campgrounds that have pools, Wi-Fi, restaurants, and playgrounds. Another option is "boondocking" or off the grid camping. This can include parking lots not generally used for motorhomes (Walmart has a company policy of allowing RVs to park in their parking lots at night) or anywhere in the undeveloped natural environment. Boondocking is the way to go for budget travelers who want to avoid campground fees and want solitude in the natural environment.

Boondocking Safety

- Make sure gas, water, propane, and batteries are full to avoid getting stuck far away from essential services.
- Carry printed maps as cell phone signals are not consistent in the backcountry.
- Make sure you have enough black and grey water storage capacity.
- Emergency medical kit, since you'll be far from a hospital.
- Reliable citizens band (CB) or emergency radio.
- Give your car a complete check over, so your trip won't be ruined by car troubles.

Preparing the Car or Recreational Vehicle (RV)

- Make any pending repairs that would impact your safety or the car's reliability.
- Check coolant levels.
- Check the oil.
- Check the battery.
- Make sure you have a spare tire and tools to change a tire, if needed.

- Check the tire pressure.
- Check all the lights and fuses.
- Check the window wipers.
- Check for leaks on your tires or anything else that could cause a flat tire or affect your safety.
- Check the engine and all the hoses for leaks.
- If you're going where it snows, bring snow chains.
- Clear out any unnecessary items sitting in your vehicle or trunk to reduce vehicle weight, save gas, and to give you more room.
- Chargers for electronics you'll be using during the trip.
- Cell phone or GPS holder, so you're not looking down while driving.
- Check registration and car insurance information is up to date, and make sure you have a copy in the vehicle.
- If you're going to be driving over long open distances and you think you might drift above the speed limit, buy a police radar detector to help you avoid police speed traps and possible tickets.
- If you're not using GPS, then you'll need maps.
- Music or audiobooks for the drive programmed into your smartphone or MP3 player.

RV Safety

- In RVs make sure you distribute the weight of items evenly throughout the vehicle; otherwise, the RV will tilt, increase your chances of a rollover, and cause excessive wear on the tires carrying the extra weight.
- If you're going to tow a vehicle, make sure your RV has the towing capacity. Not all RVs can tow a car or a storage vehicle.
- Don't drive at night. Decreased visibility increases your chances of an accident. This will help to avoid roadkill and damaging your vehicle due to debris like shredded semi-truck tires on the road.
- Test smoke and carbon monoxide detectors in your RV.
- Don't cook food while the RV is in motion.

- Buy roadside assistance insurance, such as AAA.
- If you're traveling to bear country, don't leave food or garbage around the campsite.
- If you're traveling long distances, consider whether your vehicle may need some oil or coolant, and pack it.
- Pack greywater treatment solution for your RV.

Food and Clothing:

- Use the clothing listed in the packing section of this book for suggestions.
- Snacks that can be eaten with one hand while driving: fruit, nuts, bite-size crackers and cookies, trail mix, cereal and protein bars.
- Plan ahead and buy all the food to cook your meals if you're going to stay somewhere in the middle of nowhere.

Eight Tips for Car Camping

When car camping, follow the Leave No Trace principles, and never sleep in a vehicle with the engine or AC running. Sleeping with the engine running can cause suffocation from car exhaust (carbon monoxide) leaking into the cabin.

If you're in a city, park away from neighborhoods and avoid private parking lots, or the property owners or police may knock on your window. It's best to park in industrial areas; Walmart, and some churches allow people to use their parking lots for car camping.

You can also try applications like Allstays and Hipcamp, which tell you where you can legally park and not be bothered. They give information on a variety of free and paid locations to camp for the night. The U.S. Forest Service roads are available for overnight parking and camping as long as you aren't blocking the way for others, and display any required passes or permits as indicated. Set up camp in a flat, shaded spot, aim to blend in, and avoid crowding other campers staying nearby.

The larger the vehicle, the more comfortable you're going to be. The ideal car to sleep in would have seats that fold down so you can lie flat. Sleep with your head toward the front of the vehicle.

If you're not able to find a flat location to park and you're at an angle, make sure to position the car, so your head is above your feet. Sleeping with your head to the front of the vehicle will give you more space since most cars have wheel wells at the back that take up space.

If you're going to sleep sitting up in a seat, recline your position as much as you can and, if possible, take a short walk during the night as needed. Sleeping with your feet below your heart causes your heart to have to work harder to circulate your blood. Sleeping sitting up will cause swelling in your lower extremities as your body relaxes and blood gets trapped there due to gravity. I've seen patients who have developed ulcers on their heels, varicose veins, blood clots, and even decubitus ulcers (bed sores) on their tail bones or hips from sleeping for too much time in their cars.

1. Keeping electronics charged. Remember, you can only plug in devices while the motor is running, not at night, or you'll drain your battery. Dashboard solar panels or battery banks are suitable for keeping your phone, tablet, camera, and any other electronics charged during your trip.

2. Bring an ice cooler for meats, cheese, eggs, milk, and any other perishables.

3. Use a quality mattress, pillows, and blankets. The mattress will prevent the metal car frame from pushing up against your body when you sleep. Cars get as cold as tents at night, so pack quality linens and/or a temperature-rated sleeping bag.

4. Create your own movie theater. Just make sure to download the movies on to your electronic devices before going out to areas that have weak or no Wi-Fi or cellular service.

5. Bring a battery-powered light for reading at night.

6. Stay clean. If you're sleeping in your car, you probably won't have access to sinks and showers. Keep your hygiene up with items that don't need much water like no-rinse shampoo and hand sanitizer. Bring an extra gallon of water for washing your face and brushing your teeth at night. Portable solar water showers are also useful for showering on the road.

7. Breathing all night in your car will fog up the windows, signal to others that you're sleeping in your car, and attracts unwanted attention. Leave windows slightly opened to ventilate. Open them just enough so that an animal or a person can't get in. Get window screen and cut it 2–3 inches wider than the opening. Stuff the screen around the edges of the car door to keep out the bugs.

8. Block out sensory stimulation, so you can relax. Use earplugs for noise, windshield sun shades to keep the sun out and for privacy, and a sleep mask to keep light out of your eyes.

Outdoor Camping Tips

The tent is the center of your campsite. Practice pitching your tent before you go on your trip. You must know how to set up your tent quickly and efficiently. When looking for a place to set up your tent, pick an area that has a "natural bed" of soft, flat soil; avoid the bottom of hills or valleys where water can drain into your tent. Always set up a tarp below your tent to prevent damage or water-logging.

Dress in layers. It's the easiest and most effective way to control your body temperature. Use a GPS or map and compass. No matter how familiar you are with a particular area, getting lost among acres of similar-looking trees is very easy. Learn and practice basic outdoor skills such as using and sharpening a utility knife, tying various knots, and building a fire.

Another option while camping is to go "Glamping"

(glamour + camping), a style of camping with luxury amenities and resort-style services not usually associated with "traditional" camping. Glamping can range from five-star hotel suites installed in a spectacular outdoor setting to simply elevating your car camping set up, so it feels more like a cozy home. Glamping is an excellent way to introduce someone to camping or to celebrate a special occasion.

What to Bring on a Camping Trip

- Tent, tarp, and sleeping bag
- Pot, pan, cups, dishes, utensils, scouring pad (for cleaning), and fire-starting materials (preferably waterproof matches or a butane lighter)
- Utility knife and rope
- Gallons of water for cooking and cleaning
- Easily prepared foods and snacks (pasta, beans, peanut butter, trail mix, and oatmeal), ice cooler
- Two to three layers of clothing
- Hand sanitizer and soap
- Outdoor gear depending on your hobbies (fishing poles and hiking equipment)

Chapter 10.

Travel Hygiene

Moroccan Style Home in Palm Springs California

Toilet Hygiene

Bucket of Water

A water bucket is used throughout Southeast Asia with a dipper, that is called tabo in the Philippines. It's the tool to clean the anal area, bathe, and rinse the bathroom floor.

In India, there's a floor level squat toilet with a community bucket full of water next to it from which you scoop up water with a dipper and splash on your anus, meanwhile, using your left-hand fingers to rub free any fecal matter. If you're lucky, there will be a faucet from which you can get water (not necessarily clean water) running into the bucket for you to perform the same action.

Another technique is for the user to rise up slightly from the toilet and pour water towards the small of the back where the space between the butt cheeks is. The water naturally flows down and over the skin and washes the area. This usually leads to the restroom areas to be wet and slippery, so don't be surprised to see the floors flooded all the time.

The Bidet

A shallow type of sink installed next to a regular toilet, that one squats over to wash the genital and anus region. These usually have hot/cold running water and can squirt, rinse and spray into the anus area, causing any debris from toileting to wash free. Some folks may also supplement with soap. Bidets are common in southern European countries. In northern European countries, the handheld bidet sprayer is standard in Finland and Estonia.

The Electronic Bidet Toilet Seat

Basically, a bidet integrated into the existing toilet seat. These devices, controlled with the push of a button, are designed to wash and then dry the area without the user leaving the seat. Some are simple, and some are full of hi-tech features. Japan is famous for its "smart toilets."

The Bidet Shower Spray

The handheld bidet sprayer, which is called shattaf (sounds like shit off, which is what it does) in the Middle East, is also commonly used in Southeast Asia and South Asia as a simple and effective way to clean the anal and genital areas. It connects to the water inlet valve for the toilet via a T-connection. Room temperature water is sprayed on the anus after the business is done. As with the tabo, handwashing the area with soap is an unmentioned option. The downside to using a handheld shower spray in a colder climate is that the tap water can be frigid in winter. But, if your bathroom is in Thailand or Saudi Arabia, to name a few places, you will probably have a hand shower next to the toilet, and the water won't be a cold shock.

In Muslim households, handheld bidets are very popular and are often called Muslim showers, because the Muslims are quite particular about anal and genital hygiene. The bidet shower spray is also gaining popularity in the rest of the world.

These handheld showers are often also called diaper sprayers or nappy sprayers because they can also be used to wash off most of the baby poop from your baby's diaper before tossing it in the bleach pail. The baby poo just goes right down the loo.

The Sprayer Pipe

In Egypt, you are likely to see a curved brass pipe at the back of the toilet bowl. This is water spraying at its most basic. Just turn on the tap, and a jet of water shoots towards the butt for hands-free washing, or manually assisted soaping, like with the tabo.

This is a topic not many of us want to discuss, but it's evident that the Eastern way of cleaning is the most hygienic way of doing so, although most Western cultures see these activities as uncivilized. Whichever route you choose, as long as you wash your hands afterward with soap and water, you'll decrease your risk of infections.

Places to Shower While Traveling

Sink Showers

Finding a shower or bathtub is not always possible, especially if you're camping, working outdoors, or find yourself temporarily homeless. If you have access to clean running water, taking a "bird bath" can keep you smelling fresh, looking good, and feeling your best. It might not be the most comfortable or most accessible way to clean yourself, but you will feel better than not having bathed at all.

Splash warm water on your face and neck, lather the soap and wash your face and neck, either with a wet washcloth or with your hands.

Soak the washcloth in lukewarm water and gently wring it. Rub the washcloth all over your body to moisten your skin.

Lather the soap and apply it to your body, focusing on places that tend to collect bacteria, such as the underarm area, inner thighs, genital area, buttocks and behind your ears.

Rinse the washcloth, wring it, and scrub your body with it, making sure you get all the soap off your skin. Rinse the washcloth again, twist it, and repeat as necessary. Dry yourself off with a towel.

Fill the plastic cup with warm water and turn off the faucet. Bend over the sink, making sure your head is close to the bottom of the basin. Pour the water over your head. Repeat until your hair is very wet. Apply shampoo, lather, rinse by pouring a cup of warm water over your hair, and repeat with the conditioner. Towel-dry your hair or use a hairdryer.

Items Needed:

- Tall plastic cup
- Bar of soap or liquid soap
- Towel
- Washcloth
- Shampoo
- Conditioner (optional)
- Bath towel
- Hairdryer (optional)

Department Stores

These are excellent places to wash up in the bathroom, then head for samples at the cosmetics section where you can get make up, cologne, samples, etc.

Community Colleges

Community colleges usually have open dressing rooms where you can walk in and take a shower.

Washing Clothes

The Aloksak Bag

The Aloksak is a heavy-duty ziplock bag that comes in various sizes. The bags are known for their durability and protection against the elements: air, humidity, water, dust, and sand. But they are also lightweight and easy to pack.

A 16" x 24" bag is the most convenient size to do laundry while traveling. To use the bag for washing laundry: first, throw in a fistful of detergent, add the clothes, fill the bag with hot water, and stir for five minutes with your hand. Back and forth like the blades inside a washing machine.

Then, zip the bag shut and let the clothes soak in soapy water for about ten/fifteen minutes. To rinse, either refill the bag with fresh water or use a sink. The same Aloksak bag can also be used for storing your dirty clothes.

Washing in a Sink

The sink method is not complicated. Plug the sink drain, add the detergent, and fill the sink with hot water. Hand wash your clothes. It's the most convenient way for travelers to clean their garments. There are universal drain stoppers available for travelers. You can also use a rolled-up sock to plug the drain.

Let dirty clothes soak in soapy water overnight. Afterward, scrub the clothes, rinse them in the sink, and wring them as dry as possible before hanging them to dry.

Drying Your Clothes

Whether you're washing clothes in the Aloksak bag or in the sink, finding a fast, efficient way to dry them is crucial.

If it's sunny, and your guesthouse or hostel has a clothesline outside, often on the roof, line drying in the fresh air only takes a few hours.

However, if it's raining, or no outside clothesline is available, there's a way to speed things up. Get a dry towel, spread it on the bed, place a garment on the towel, and roll it up tight. The towel will absorb some additional moisture, and your clothes will dry faster when you hang them inside on a rope or an elastic laundry line for travelers.

Coin-Operated Laundromats

Coin-operated laundromats or launderettes can be found all over the world in larger towns and cities. Sometimes even hostels or guesthouses will have a few washers and dryers. Many of them also offer Wi-Fi connections. Great for meeting people!

Local Laundry Houses

In some countries, there is usually a family-run laundry operation within walking distance in every neighborhood. Your clothes are weighed to determine the price. Sometimes machine drying is available, which is faster but more expensive, and they can have your clothes washed and dried in a few hours! Line drying in the sun is conventional but takes longer. An overnight wait is typical.

Recycling or Re-wearing Clothes

To help reduce the amount of laundry, you can wear the same pants and shirts for a few days until they start looking and feeling dirty. Wearing your clothes until they are actually soiled makes sense if you are on the move and want to save time. This strategy won't work if you're somewhere tropical where you are sweating a lot.

Chapter 11.

Traveling Solo, in Groups, for Business, Staycation, or Gap Year Travel

Birthday with Friends from All over the Planet

Solo Travelers

My friend Stanley told me a story about his mom traveling to Venice, Italy, when she was in her early seventies. While sightseeing, she met an Italian woman around the same age who was well dressed, well mannered, and charming. The two started talking and hit it off. They decided to have lunch in a nice restaurant where they could continue talking. After their delicious Italian meal, the woman excused herself to go to the restroom and never came back! Stanley said his mom was fond of this memory and mentioned it often during the rest of her life into her eighties before she passed away. The point of this story is that being alone makes you more approachable, which can be useful for making friends, but also exposes you to undesirables, so you have to be alert.

Although traveling solo may seem scary, you are more likely to get bumped, upgraded, or allowed to join groups of other people. When you are alone, you are never outnumbering or intimidating, which makes it easier to join in with others. You will make friends faster, and you can decide to stay as long or as little as you like in the company of your new friends. Leave off the headphones to increase approachability.

While in Nepal, I was desperately trying to book a tour to Bhutan for the next day—which is the only way to get into the country due to its travel restrictions—since I was only there for a few days and had not made any prior arrangements. The tour groups were all fully booked for two weeks out, but I kept asking until I found an operator who had a group of Chinese tourists headed to Bhutan. The group had one empty seat available and was willing to include an American in their group. These people were really friendly and asked me questions throughout our trip. They were extremely curious about American culture. I found the experience very enriching since I had seven people always asking me about my country, sharing stories, and reflecting on the differences in our perceptions. At every sight we were visiting, each one of them would line up to take a solo picture with me. They seemed very proud to have an American friend with them, as was I to have the opportunity to share the experience with these kind folks. Bhutan was terrific, but the time I shared with the group of middle-aged friends from China was even more rewarding.

Group Travel

Going on a trip with a group of friends or family can be a remarkable and unforgettable experience. But in practice, it can be tough agreeing on details, and can often result in disagreements over hotels and the itinerary. The key is to be relaxed, patient, flexible with whatever comes up, and to be a team player. Be on time, don't make the others wait or the group is not going to appreciate you. Avoid conversations that are tenuous like politics or religion. Communicate so everyone is clear about what the objectives are. Be democratic, so everyone feels they have a say in all matters; typically, it is the majority that rules. Plan out all the details in advance, so there are fewer decisions to make and less unexpected changes that someone may not agree with.

If this all sounds like too much, then consider signing up with a tour group that will handle all of the logistics for you and make things a lot easier for everyone to agree to.

Higher priced resorts are also a good option as they have a lot of the details worked out for you ahead of time, such as meals, and most of them have a variety of activities available for guests.

If you decide to plan the trip yourself, I would recommend renting a house on Airbnb or HomeAway. Renting a house can save you money and create a pleasant environment. That way, no one can hide out in their hotel room. Renting a house allows you to cook together, eat together, and just sit and talk as much as you like. You can buy groceries in advance using PeaPod or Amazon Pantry, so everything is waiting for you when you arrive at the house.

I booked a trip to Cancún for a group of ten for ten days, which was one of the best trips I've ever taken. The hotels were running around $100 a night, and I would have had to reserve three rooms. Instead, we rented a four-bedroom house for sixteen people on Airbnb for $40 a night. We rented a twelve-seater van for $35 a day, and we found some buffets out by the pyramids for $2 a person with traditional Mayan dancers included. The most important lesson I learned was not to be overly ambitious as everyone slept different schedules, ate at different speeds, and took different amounts of time to get ready. The best part was just hanging out together cooking, chopping veggies, eating, everyone cooking their favorite dishes to share, talking, playing games, and planning our outings together. The time just seemed to fly by as we enjoyed being interwoven in each other's company.

How to Save Money While on Tour

In Los Angeles, we have a creative culture and traveling as part of a band, film crew, or art installation frequently requires going on tour. Touring is an unforgettable experience; if not planned out properly, it can cost you and your bandmates thousands and dampen the experience. Aside from the other recommendations in this book, here are some specific tips for artists.

1. Housing: Hotels can be expensive, and the more you spend, the less time you'll be able to spend on tour. Reach out to family, friends, fans, hosting venues, and other artists you'll be working with to share spaces and crash with them for free.

2. Food and Drink: Eating out and drinking at clubs can be costly. Instead of spending $12 on a beer at a venue, buy yourself a six-pack for $3 and make yourself some sandwiches to eat out in the parking lot before going in. It doesn't sound very cool, but again the goal is to be able to afford to finish the tour; any artist will tell you that to be successful, you have to sacrifice.

3. Attend as many venues as you can: Plan on performing your craft as much as possible in as many shows as you can in the shortest amount of time possible. The Beatles used to perform up to three times a day (often free) to survive and develop their musical skills. The more time you spend filming, performing, or creating, the better you're going to get at your art, and the more money you'll be able to make selling merchandise and playing shows. To achieve this goal, book as many shows as you can close

together to save on travel expenses and be able to schedule as many shows as possible. Smaller cities tend to be easier to work in, the people tend to be more welcoming, and thanks to social media, they can often give you the same amount of exposure.

4. Follow a plan: Make a budget with your team, allocate money for food, gas, housing, and all other expenses (check out the budget section for tips). Be open and discuss everything with your team before the trip, discuss if any profits will be split between group members, reinvested into new equipment, future tours, or maintenance on the team vehicle. Finances can often be a point of contention, so lay everything out beforehand, so everyone knows what to expect. Also, discuss unexpected expenses and how to cover them, including your vehicle breaking down, someone getting sick, or not generating enough money to get back home from tour. Make a contingency plan to address these issues and sign a written agreement with your team, so things don't end in dispute, and prevent the possibility of being able to undertake a similar journey again and further your artistic careers.

Staycation

Staycation ("stay" and "vacation") or holistay ("holiday" and "stay"), is when an individual or family stays at home participating in leisure activities within driving distance of their home that don't require overnight accommodations. Staycations help reduce anxiety, stress, and the financial restraints of travel abroad.

Eight Suggestions for Staycations:

1. Plan as if you were leaving out of town. You and your travel partners should clear your schedules of work, chores, and other commitments so that you can be as free as possible to live like vacationers. Having an open schedule will give you the freedom to enjoy your time as if you were really on vacation.

2. Get a travel guidebook and a map, which will expose

you to new places and experiences in your neighborhood, even if you've lived there your whole life.

3. Take a walking tour: Traveling on foot will allow you to see things you may not have ever noticed while driving in your car. Walking will allow you to soak in the surrounding environment, observe the people, and access new places.

4. Look for day trips in your area: Drive routes you've never driven before; visit cultural sites, parks, activities, other tourist attractions you always wanted to see.

5. Pretend your home is a hotel room. When you're on vacation, you don't hang out in your hotel room; you stay out all day enjoying the sites. Don't go home until you're ready to go to bed.

6. Spend time with the special people in your life. If your typical schedule does not allow you to interact as much as you'd like with family and friends, then set some time aside to reconnect. Schedule outings with friends, dinners, activities, or host a get-together. Enjoying time with people you care for can be much more rewarding than traveling somewhere far away.

7. Spend more than you usually would on food and activities. Since you're saving on hotels and airfare, spend some of those savings on activities that you might typically avoid because of cost.

8. Unplug: Minimize communication with work and avoid social media.

Business Travel

It's especially important to travel light during business trips because typically you have little free time available between work and sightseeing, so you don't want to squander valuable time on managing luggage.

Do as much preparation and research as you can before your trip to help save time. Outline a plan of what you would like to see before you get there. If you have limited time, go for the must-see places first. Use your time wisely; go sightseeing before dinner or during a lunch break; eat while you tour around, etc. Try combining elements of your pleasure trip with your business trip so you can deduct part of your journey from your taxes.

Quick Business List:

- Maintain a bag ready to go with the essentials so you can get up and go quickly.
- Pack light. Use some of the previously mentioned suggestions in the packing section.
- Avoid checking bags since these trips may be short. You don't want to waste time waiting for lost or delayed luggage.
- Bring items that can be used up while on your trip so the empty space can be filled on the way back with things you are bringing home.
- Make sure you are getting miles for as many aspects of your trip as you can: rental cars, meals, tickets, and all purchases.

Gap Year Travel

A gap year is usually time off between high school and college. The difference between a vacation and a gap year is that the gap year may last any length of time, up to a year or more. A gap year can be life-changing. Spending time living abroad nurtures creativity, opens your mind, and will unlock a life full of adventure.

A gap year may involve a variety of things like backpacking, time out between careers, a short gap year, or a sabbatical. A gap year can be valuable time spent between life stages; traveling, volunteering, and working abroad, or doing all three.

While staying in an ashram in India, I met several people on a gap year vacation from around the world. The dorms were twenty cents a night, and the meals were eight cents. So, for forty-four cents you could cover your meals and housing for a day. These types of prices allow people who are going through divorces, breakups, career changes, traumatic life experiences, breaks from school, or just about any other situation a person might go through, to take a gap year and recalibrate. I've met people in Southeast Asia, Mexico, and Africa having such experiences.

Because of the low prices, people can stay away for extended periods of time and merely reset. I've met some fascinating people who were in unfortunate life situations. Many had tried therapy without making any progress, and the only way they were able to overcome their circumstances was to get away. If you're going through a rough patch in your life, I would seriously recommend taking a gap year to heal yourself. As a clinician of twenty years and who has worked with thousands of people, I've hardly ever seen anything more effective.

Chapter 12.

Twenty Ways to Blend in Anywhere

Mingling with a Tribe in Kenya Africa

Wherever you go, people will be as interested in you as you are in them. Therefore, you should try to blend in as much as possible so you can see them in their natural state, and you can benefit from the experience of traveling to that location. You also want to keep yourself safe, and the more you can blend in, the safer you are from criminals.

1. Wear clothes without bright colors, labels, or advertisements, as plain and straightforward as you can find. And if your budget allows, buy a few of the local dress

items and wear those.

2. Pack clothes that are versatile and multipurpose. For example, blue jeans can be worn for hiking or dancing at a nightclub.

3. Hide all your tourist accessories in a bag or backpack, and only bring them out when necessary: items such as cameras, money pouches, binoculars, etc. Try to keep a low profile.

4. Try to wear the colors and type of clothing that the locals wear. If everyone is wearing shorts and sandals, then don't wear Levi's and Nikes.

5. Check out the weather at your travel destination so you know what types of clothing would work best with the weather.

6. Keep money in the local currency in small denominations, easily accessible so you can complete transactions quickly without showing a lot of cash. I usually carry cash in a money belt and have a dummy wallet with little cash in my pocket for daily use. If I get robbed, I just give them the dummy wallet.

7. Act as the locals do; greet as they do, sit as they do, line up as they do, and always be friendly.

8. Make a plan for the day, scope out your route, bring whatever you'll need, maps, etc. You'll run through your day more seamlessly without having to keep stopping to ask people for help.

9. Do your shopping for whatever you need where the locals do—allowing you to learn more about them and their customs. Learn how to say "I'm here for work" in the local language to help prevent locals from heckling you to buy their items and attracting attention to you.

10. Go to the places that are less visited and visit the main attractions during off-peak hours, such as early in the morning or late at night (if it's safe). If you know certain

places will be busy at certain times, go there some other time. Midday can be an excellent time to explore highly visited areas, when most people are having lunch and the places free up for a while.

11. Pick up some basic language skills for wherever you are visiting.

12. Don't be loud, keep your voice down, and if you speak in your native language, speak quietly. You don't want people hearing you speak a different language in a room, it will attract curious onlookers.

13. Stay in areas that are not crowded with tourists. This will allow you to see how the locals live and will enable you to blend in easier although tourist areas are safer if you're visiting a country that has safety concerns.

14. If you're driving, pay attention; don't stop or park in the wrong places. Try to observe as many of the local driving habits unless they're unsafe. Don't stop traffic while you look at sights or take pictures from your car.

15. Walk like you know where you're going, and look confident.

16. Talk to the locals and find out about the sights, festivals, restaurants, and activities. Sometimes new things are happening that are not in tour books or online.

17. Say hello, smile, and approach people in the street. That'll make it easier and faster to find places.

18. Try to learn a second language, preferably Spanish and/or French, and as a last resort use, Google Translate or Nicetranslator. English and Spanish are the two most commonly used languages around the world so you can usually find someone who speaks either one of them.

19. Use body language when there's a language barrier. Shouting in your own language is not going to get you far. Instead, use your body; it's the most international language.

20. Look at images on the internet of the people and the place you're about to visit. Plan your wardrobe with colors and styles to match the locals.

When visiting foreign countries, you should take full advantage of learning the culture and traditions of that country. Learning about other people's perceptions will help you understand yourself and your own culture better. As a traveler, joining in during festivals, eating local foods, observing customs and traditions will help you learn about the region you're visiting much faster. Mixing with locals, asking questions, and just doing what the locals do will improve your experience and make it that much more memorable.

Chapter 13.

Five Strategies for Working Abroad

Kennedy Space Center Florida

Working in a foreign country is the best way to learn about a culture and really immerse yourself in its customs. It's the best way to learn a language, and it allows you to meet a lot of people in different contexts. These experiences lend themselves to helping you become more adaptable; the more versatile you are, the better traveler you will become. The extra cash will also help you extend your travels and help you cover more ground for more extended periods without having to head back to your home court.

However, to be successful at having an excellent overseas work experience, it's going to take some planning to find better jobs. This allows you to work out the issues regarding language barriers, work permits, or visa requirements. If you just show up, you're likely to find a lower-paying job and be limited to seasonal work, teaching a language in a non-traditional setting, or trading your labor for room and board.

English is the universal language; therefore, there are many more opportunities for English speakers, although there are opportunities for people who speak other languages as well. There are many resources online for finding jobs teaching languages worldwide.

If you're an English-speaking traveler, you can apply in your home country for a visa to work on a work holiday assignment in English speaking countries. These visas are valid for about a year, and you can't work in one place for more than six months at a time. These are good for people taking time off from school or between jobs.

These jobs are usually in the service industry and are not often very well paid, but they are enough to support you and help you save money to keep traveling. I've met people who travel for a few months, then work a few months in Australia, New Zealand, Canada, or England. They save up some money, then go for another few months. They can go back and forth for years and years making a life of working and traveling for the rest of their lives.

If you are a professional, these jobs take even more planning and time to land as you have to meet the visa, language, and professional requirements for the country where you are trying to work. For these jobs, it is recommended to go with an agency that can place you much faster and help you navigate the requirements more rapidly. If you happen to be a healthcare professional, this is an even easier road to travel.

Strategies to find gigs overseas

- The most important thing is to implement these strategies from your home country before you travel, not when you get there.

- Invest time looking for jobs.
- Learn about the requirements for the countries where you want to work.
- Contact expats and friends.
- Apply online through agencies and employment websites.
- Have your credentials ready.

Chapter 14.

Family Travel

Hanging with the family in Chichen Itza Mexico

Kids

Bring stuff to keep them busy on flights. Or, if you are facing a big-time difference, you can adjust to sleeping time at home to help lessen the change.

Scheduling Flights

For example, if you have a three-hour flight, try to schedule it during your child's nap time, so they sleep through the trip. That way, you will be able to enjoy the flight.

Seat Assignments

Request bulkhead seating so there won't be people sitting in front of you for your child to bump into. Bassinets are usually in this area as well, but confirm since there are not bassinets in all bulkhead seating areas.

The SeatGuru application allows you to check the best seats for kids on a model of the plane, the location of bassinets and bathrooms, what types of outlets they have, to help you choose your seats.

Prepare your child for the trip, tell them what to expect and what you'll be doing at the airport. Reading children's books about flying and travel is an excellent way to start.

Plan for Extra Time at the Airport

Get there early so you can check-in, go through security, feed and change your child before the flight, so you are not rushed or stressed.

If you are breastfeeding, feed your child at takeoff and landing. This will help their ears adjust to the cabin pressure.

If your child is eating solid foods, try to do so before boarding, so the movement does not jar baby food out of your hands.

Read the TSA's Traveling with Kids Section

https://www.tsa.gov/traveler-information/traveling-children

Use a collapsible stroller so you can check it in at the gate, and it'll be available for you at landing. You won't have to carry your child to the baggage claim.

Trunki, multipurpose luggage for children that can also be used as a footrest, seat, and a cart for your child to sit on when they are tired. You can pull them through the airport.

Bring some cleansing wipes with you. As soon as you sit down, wipe down the area within reach of your child to help ensure everything is clean for him/her.

Before takeoff, gather all the essentials you will need for your child in the first thirty minutes or so, snacks, toys, etc.

Sippy or straw cups: keep the lid loose, so the pressure does not build-up due to the cabin pressure. Otherwise, when you open it, the liquid will spray everywhere. Make sure you have liquids available for your child during the flight to avoid "Daddy, I'm thirsty."

Age-appropriate Tylenol can be used to relieve ear pressure. Although a much better and healthier alternative is to have your child breastfeed or munch on snacks at takeoff and landing. Lollipops are a good option as they last a long time.

Etiquette

Make sure your child is not bothering other passengers, lifting the tray table up and down, kicking seats, running in the aisles, etc.

Diapers

Bring extras in case of delays. Some airlines stock diapers as a courtesy, but they may not have your child's size. It's always good to bring your own changing mat to make sure you have a clean surface to lay your baby on and leave the surface you are using clean after changing your baby on the plane.

Bring diaper disposal bags to throw away diapers, and bring baby powder to douse the inside of waste diapers, so you don't smell the place up for other passengers.

Use extra diaper cream to avoid your child getting a diaper rash during long flights. Your child will be sitting in their diaper for much longer than they are accustomed. Diaper rashes are common for flying babies if you don't take precautions.

You may have to change a diaper at your seat during emergencies, like when the seat belt light is on, which is more reason to bring scented diaper disposal bags with you.

Warming bottles and food. If you ask the attendant to warm your food, test it first, as it may be too hot for your child.

Baby Food

Baby formula, breast milk, and juice for infants or toddlers are permitted above the typical 3.4-ounce limit—in reasonable quantities—through the airline security checkpoint. Remove these items from your carry-on bag to be screened separately from the rest of your belongings. Inform the TSA officer at the beginning of the screening process that you carry formula, breast milk, and juice above 3.4 ounces in your carry-on bag. These liquids are typically screened by X-ray. The Food and Drug Administration states that there are no known adverse effects from eating food, drinking beverages, and using medicine screened by X-ray.

TSA officers may need to test liquids for explosives or concealed prohibited items. Officers may ask you to open the container and/or have you transfer a small quantity of the liquid to a separate empty container or dispose of a small amount, if feasible. Inform the TSA officer if you do not want the formula, breast milk, and/or juice to be X-rayed or opened. Additional steps will be taken to clear liquid, and you or the traveling guardian will undergo additional screening procedures, including a pat-down and screening of other carry-on property.

Bring your own baby food. Airlines often offer canned baby food, but you don't know what kind, and you don't want your baby to have an allergic reaction or an upset stomach during the flight.

You have to request child meals in advance, or you won't get any. They typically include juice boxes, smaller utensils, and kid-friendly snacks.

Child Travel Items

- Snacks: bring plenty of them. You don't want a hungry child on a flight. Don't bring snacks that smell. Bring satiating snacks. Limit sugar so your kids won't be bouncing off the walls.
- Onboard entertainment: bring everything you can to keep your kids entertained. If you don't allow TV at home, now is the time to break that rule; bring iPad with movies, applications, and extra batteries.
- In case of a meltdown, wrap inexpensive gifts or treats, and present them during meltdowns.
- Sleeping: ask your doctor if children's Benadryl is okay to use to help your child sleep during long flights.
- If your child has a special blanket or doll that he/she sleeps with, bringing it along will help him/her rest better.
- When you get to your destination, try to keep the same routine for your children's nap times, eating, bathing, etc. If they decide to sleep beyond their regular sleep times, wake them up and stick to the usual schedule.
- Saline spray is good to use when the children's noses are dry to avoid nosebleed and/or discomfort.
- When flying alone overseas, it's a good idea to bring a notarized letter from your partner, giving you permission to travel with your children. Not that they ask very often, but that is the rule for international travel with children.
- To help keep kids busy during flights. Airlines offer freebies for kids, such as toys, child-friendly toiletry kits, meals, and kid-friendly entertainment.

Chapter 15.

Travel Safety

Snorkeling with Sea Urchins in the Red Sea Egypt

Travel Scenarios

Don't assume places away from your home are more dangerous. Keep an open mind to new experiences, and don't view things that are different as unsafe.

During a trip to Ecuador with my sister Patricia, we decided to change our travel plans and head to Colombia, although we were both terrified to go there because of all the Pablo Escobar narco stories and the paramilitary kidnappings. We assumed there was a strong possibility we might not make it out alive, but we really wanted to go.

We started out by riding a bus full of people to the Colombian border from Ecuador's capital of Quito. It was a long bus ride that ended up with only me and my sister left on the bus. We were dropped off on a dirt road about a mile from the border and told to walk. Apparently, Ecuador and Colombia had political differences, and people were avoiding the border crossing. We interpreted this as a sign of severe danger. Patricia and I walked up to the utterly deserted border crossing and shouted for someone to come out.

After a twelve-hour trip, we were worried the border was closed; we couldn't see anyone. After a few minutes, a door opened, and two border agents came out dressed in plain clothes. They seemed surprised to see us, and that made us feel uneasy. I asked them if it was a good idea to travel to Colombia. One of the men seemed annoyed by the question and asked us, "Why?" I answered, "Well, because of all the kidnappings and drug wars."

He asked, "Is your country like the movie, Die Hard, where terrorists are blowing up skyscrapers and driving buses into malls?" I answered, "Of course not." He said, "Exactly. Don't believe everything you see on television." That simple analogy made us feel much better, and so we crossed into Colombia. We did see banners posted in most of the major cities demanding that the government retrieve kidnapped citizens, but other than that, it was like most developing countries: full of new things to see and friendly people. We simply used common sense and toured the country from coast to coast. It was one of our favorite trips together, full of awesome memories.

Safe Air Travel

Air travel is generally safe, but here are some tips for increased safety. Try to take nonstop flights. The fewer connections, the less likely you are to crash. Most crashes happen during takeoff or landing. The odds of surviving a plane crash are higher if you're sitting in the back of the plane. The safest seat is a window seat in the emergency aisle, because you'll be the first one out the door in case of a crash.

It is essential to listen to the flight attendants when they're reviewing safety information. Know where your flotation device is located and how to use it. In case of an emergency, follow the directions of the flight crew. Keep alcohol to a minimum on flights; alcohol will decrease your mobility and reaction time during an emergency. Alcohol also has a stronger effect on you when you're in a pressurized cabin versus being on the ground.

Muggers

Don't fight or argue over material things. Just hand them over. It's not worth your life. If it's clear that they are going to hurt you, then aim to do severe damage and disable them in one blow.

- Poke them as hard as you can in the eyes.
- Hit or squeeze their balls if they are male.
- Elbow them in the ribs.
- Drive your knee into their groin.
- Strike their throat with a chopping motion or punch them in the throat.
- If you have a key or a stick, aim for the eyes. Hold the key between your fingers and hit their face.

If you forget everything else then just SING; stands for an elbow to the **s**olar plexus (guts), stomp the **i**nstep (foot), elbow to the **n**ose, and punch to the **g**roin.

How to Escape Fast Moving Water

If you fall in the water, ride the current on your back with your head pointing upstream and your feet pointing downstream. This will allow you to push off from rocks or other obstacles with your feet as you approach them. Don't try to stand up, the water may carry you into something and cause you more damage.

As the river bends, look for calm patches of water and try to move towards them. Don't swim straight towards the shore or the water will carry you away, swim in a forty-five-degree angle towards the shoreline.

If you're stuck in stronger and deeper rapids, float on your stomach instead. This will allow you to have your arms out front to protect your head and face. Time your breathing; take a deep breath in between each wave. If you get pulled under for an extended period, don't panic, it happens. Just wait for the current to pull you back up out of the water. Meanwhile, protect your face and neck with your hands.

When you're floating, keep your body horizontal to the surface. This reduces the risk of you being sucked under by a current.

Bed Bugs

Bedbugs are flat, round, reddish-brown, and about a quarter inch (7 millimeters) in length. Bedbugs can't fly or jump and lurk in cracks and crevices, but they aren't known to transmit disease or pose any serious medical risk. They can leave itchy, bumpy red, and unsightly bites. If they don't have a food source, they can live up to two years in hibernation and wake up as soon as they sense movement from a possible food source. Bedbugs will hide in the seams and folds of luggage, bags, clothes, behind wallpaper, inside bedding, box springs, and furniture.

Six Tips for Avoiding Bed Bugs

1. When you arrive in your hotel room, head directly to the restroom and place your bags in the shower.

2. Before bringing your luggage into the bedroom, use a flashlight to check the mattress's seams and all sides of the box spring.

3. Once the coast is clear, place your bags on top of tables, do not put your suitcase on the bed. It's best never to put your luggage on the bed. It will reduce the chances of bed bugs getting into your luggage.

4. Be vigilant, bed bugs can travel through the walls from room to room.

5. To be sure, wash all of your belongings to help ensure you're not bringing bed bugs back home because they can hide in your clothes or suitcase.

6. After you wash all of your belongings, seal your bags in plastic to keep the bugs out.

Scorpion Stings

- Remain calm, unless you are allergic to them. Most scorpion bites won't hurt you.
- Apply heat or cold packs for pain relief.
- For allergic reactions, take an antihistamine
- The pain is most severe at the sting site.
- Watch for tingling or pain in the limbs.
- Take pain medication, if available.
- Scorpions are generally not deadly. A tourniquet can cause more harm than good.
- Don't cut and suck the wound like they do in the movies. That will spread the venom and do more harm.
- Scorpions like to seek refuge in shoes, towels, or linens, so inspect them if you are in an area where scorpions are prevalent.

How to Remove a Leech

Don't burn, squeeze, use salt, or spray insect repellent. This will only cause regurgitation, which will give you an infection. Look for the smaller end of the leech, slide your nail sideways under its mouth, and flick the leech off. Leeches hang out in shallow water and can sense heat and vibrations.

How to Survive Bear Attacks

- Avoid eye contact, as bears will perceive this as a threat, or you'll provoke them to attack.
- Don't climb trees. All bears can climb trees faster than humans.
- Don't try to run. Bears run faster than humans. They assume you're a prey and chase you down.
- If you're traveling in an area with bears, you should carry bear pepper spray. It's made specifically for bears, so don't buy the spray for dogs or humans.
- If a bear charges you, just stand your ground; don't

run. Sometimes bears will charge just to see what you will do, then they stop before they reach you.

- If it's a black bear, make noise and fight back with your fists. Most black bears will get scared away by the sound of a large person yelling. Don't play dead.
- If it's a brown or a grizzly bear attacking you, drop to the ground, roll into a fetal position, and cover your neck with your hands. The bears will move on, once they see you're not a threat.
- Polar bears are some of the few animals that will prey on humans. Other predators such as lions and sharks will attack in defense, but are not generally interested in eating human flesh. Don't go into polar bear areas without pepper spray, which is much more effective (98%) than firearms (76%). Also, take precautions as polar bears are the biggest and most dangerous of all bears.
- If any type of bear is following you, then you're going to be attacked as prey by the bear. In this case, fighting would be your only option.

How to Survive Shark Attacks

You're more likely to be struck by lightning than being attacked by a shark. Most sharks are not dangerous, except for bull, tiger, and great white sharks.

Avoid areas where people or boats are fishing. The blood from the bait and cleaning fish attracts the sharks.

Do not urinate or bleed in shark-prone areas; sharks will swim in from miles away to investigate even a few drops. If you cut yourself, get out of the water.

Smooth swimming movements are less likely to attract sharks versus thrashing and leg kicking. It's safer to swim and surf in groups. Sharks are prone to attack loners.

Don't wear bright colors, they attract sharks. If you end up in the ocean with a bright orange or yellow life vest, take it off. Marine biologists call this yum-yum yellow.

Most shark attacks consist of one bite, and then they swim away. That's because it's a warning bite and sharks are territorial. Sharks also don't like to eat human flesh; they prefer fatty seal meat.

A shark's nose, eyes, and grill are very sensitive, so try to jab them with whatever you have to scare them away. Try not to use your hands or feet, or you may lose them.

If a shark bites you, they're most likely not coming back, so your priority should be to get out of the water as soon as possible and stop the bleeding.

Shark repellent made of fermented shark carcass is available.

How to Deal with Altitude Sickness

- The risk increases once you go past 8,000 feet.
- Acclimatize, ascend slowly, not more than 1,000 feet per day.
- The oxygen levels in your blood are lower at night, so descend to lower elevations. Do not sleep more than 2,000 feet higher than you did the night before.
- Drink twice as much water, avoid alcohol and excess exercise to avoid dehydration and lower blood oxygen levels.
- Eat foods rich in potassium, such as nuts and bananas.
- Once you pass 9,000 feet, spend an extra day acclimating for every 3,000 feet climbed.
- If you get acute mountain sickness (AMS), descend immediately in 1,500 feet chunks till your symptoms go away.
- You can take Viagra or chew on coca leaves: both are vasodilators and help with headaches, nausea, and other symptoms of AMS.

How to Survive a Drug Overdose

- If you suspect a drug overdose, act immediately. Call for emergency services before the heart stops, or the person is incapacitated and can't move.

- If the person is awake, keep them conscious by walking around with them. You can also place them under a cold shower to wake them up, just keep the water away from their mouth and nose so they can breathe.
- Don't allow a person to fall asleep; and if they do, wake them up or their heart may stop, and they'll stop breathing.
- If the person is unconscious, lay them on their side; so if they vomit, they won't aspirate, choke, and die.
- It's not highly effective, but you can try giving the overdosed person milk to drink if the person is conscious. The calcium in the milk will bind with the drugs and negate some of their effects.
- Avoid illegal drug use. If you decide to use illegal drugs, then try small doses if you're a first-time user. This will help you figure out if you're going to have a negative reaction to the drug. If you take a smaller dose, the symptoms may be manageable.

How to Survive a Tornado in a Car

- If you see a tornado, go into a building. If you can't reach one in time, drive away from the storm as fast as possible.
- If you're stuck in your car; park off the road, fasten your seatbelt, keep your head down, and cover yourself with a blanket or coat.
- Don't hide in the trunk of your car.
- If there's a ditch or hole somewhere close by that is below ground level, go lie down there and cover your neck.

How to Bribe a Police Officer or Immigration Official

- Learn the local terms for bribes; otherwise, ask if you can "pay the fine on the spot" or pay to "expedite the process." Don't be overt or the officer could get upset or offended. Be discreet.
- Never hand money to an official. Place the cash into your passport, in their ticket book or note pad, and

hand it back.

- Learn the going rate for bribes in the area, and if you don't have small enough bills, don't expect change.

How to Survive in the Desert

- Stay out of the sun. Moving around in the sun will make you sweat and cause you to dehydrate faster.
- Don't waste energy looking for food. You can live weeks without food, so it's best not to expend water looking for food.
- If you're stuck in the desert and you have a car, don't leave it. It will provide shade from the sun during the day and protection from the cold at night. It's also easier to spot the car in case someone is looking for you. If you don't have a car, then only walk at night when it's cooler.
- Look for water on the northside of canyons, gullies, or big rocks. Seeing birds and insects is also a good sign that water is nearby.
- Watch for poisonous snakes, scorpions, spiders, and insects. They will be attracted to your body heat at night, so keep your shirt tucked in your pants, pants tucked into your socks, and sleep as high off the ground as possible.
- At night lay out your jacket or tarps to collect whatever dew you can for drinking.
- Don't drink from a cactus; the fluid inside is noxious, and it'll make you vomit. It only works in movies.
- Don't drink your urine. It's concentrated waste, and drinking it will dehydrate you further. When you're dehydrated, the urine you produce is more concentrated than usual with waste and will cause you more harm. Yes, it's sterile, but the built-up waste in it can cause kidney damage.
- Be careful with dust storms, they can kill you. If you see clouds of dust moving towards you, take shelter by a large rock or anything sticking out of the ground. Cover your eyes, mouth, and nose with some fabric.

How to Survive Falling into a Waterfall

- Don't waste your time fighting the water current. It can reach speeds of up to 40 miles per hour. Instead, position yourself for the fall. Point your feet downstream, straighten out your body, lying horizontally, and your head up.
- Place your hands on your head, touch your elbows in front of your nose, close your eyes and your mouth, and take a deep breath as you fall over the waterfall.
- Before you hit the water, tighten your muscles to help prevent bones from shattering into your body and tearing tissue.
- As you hit the water, keep your toes pointed downwards, and remain vertically aligned. That will minimize the damage to your organs.
- Don't panic, you'll be disoriented. Be prepared to be submerged for a bit after you fall into the water. The water current will be strong, just flow with the water, and your body will float to the surface.
- If the water is freezing, you have about three minutes to get out of the water before it becomes lethal.
- As you swim out of the water, be careful of rocks and debris that can puncture your skin and cause more damage.

How to Survive Falling Off a Ship at Sea

- When falling from a large ship, enter feet first to help prevent head trauma and broken bones.
- Take a deep breath before hitting the water. If the water is cold, it will cause an involuntary gasping response that is produced when you suddenly enter cold water. If your lungs are not already filled with air, you'll inhale sea water, and it'll cause you to drown.
- The colder the water, the less time you'll have for the rescuers to find you before hypothermia sets in, so try to conserve heat by not swimming. Just float and keep your arms close to your body to retain heat.
- If your ship sails away, then swim towards the

closest land you can see.

- If you're on a fishing boat or some other type of high-risk boat, wear your life vest at all times. If you're in shark-filled waters, take your jacket off and allow it to float away. If you have rubber boots, they can be used to capture air and held under your arms as floatation devices.
- Twenty percent of people die when they are being rescued, because they've become incapacitated from not moving and can't muster enough energy to grab the rescue equipment. So, as the rescuers approach, start moving to get your blood flowing, and to regain your coordination.

How to Survive a Forest Fire

- Always try to run away from the fire versus taking shelter. Look up and see which way the smoke is blowing and run in the opposite direction. The direction the wind is blowing tells you which way the fire will spread the fastest.
- Run to natural firebreaks, barriers that slow down or stop the progress of fire, such as roads, rivers, lakes, or open fields.
- Don't try to outrun fires, the flames can move at 30-40 miles per hour, while the fastest runners in the world run 26 miles per hour. If you must run, run towards lower areas and areas that have already burned.
- If the fire is upon you, don't cover your mouth with a wet piece of fabric; the liquid will heat up and boil your skin. Take a deep breath and hold it till the superheated air passes over you. Inhaling it will kill you instantly.
- If you're out of options, bury yourself in the dirt with your feet facing the fire and just wait for the flames to pass over you.

How to Survive a Riot

- Try to stay indoors and wear long-sleeved shirts and long pants. This will help protect you from debris and to minimize exposure to tear gas or pepper spray if you get caught outside. Wear clothing that blend in, without bright colors or logos that attract attention. Don't wear dark clothing, hoodies, or any clothing that looks like a uniform as it can be misinterpreted by police or military. Stay calm and stay out of it. Stay up to date on what's happening. You can plan an escape route, if needed, away from the mobs.

- If you're driving, drive away from the mobs, and drive slowly so you don't attract attention.
- Walk away from problem areas. Leave your baggage behind, but carry your travel documents, cell phone, and some food with you.
- Avoid getting hit by riot control chemicals and weapons.
- Carry some toothpaste to smear under your eyes if tear gas is released.
- Bring a bandanna soaked in lemon juice or vinegar and keep it in a bag. You can breathe through it to give you some protection from the gas. Keep rinsing the bandanna as it gets saturated with gas.
- Carry a solution of half liquid antacid and half water, which can be used to rinse your eyes if you're exposed to tear gas.
- Wear glasses for eye protection, not contacts that can be very painful if tear gas gets underneath them; or wear swim goggles or a gas mask if you have any.
- Don't rub your eyes, nose, or mouth; this will spread the chemicals that may have been sprayed on you.
- If you have an extra set of clothes, carry them with you in a plastic bag so you can change in case you're hit with chemicals.
- Wear latex or vinyl gloves to protect your hands from pepper spray; getting the spray on your hands is very painful.
- Avoid wearing creams or sunblock, because chemicals can adhere to them and prolong the pain.

How to Survive a Human Stampede

135

- If you're stuck in the middle, don't move against the crowd; move in a diagonal with the flow of the crowd, the same way you would if you were being carried by a river. Stay on the perimeters of the crowd, and avoid the densest areas.
- If you fall, get up fast. If you can't get up, get on your knees and cover your head and neck with your arms.
- If you have kids, keep them on your shoulders or elevated as much as possible.
- Keep your arms up around your chest so you have some space to breathe.
- If you start getting squeezed, turn sideways, perpendicular to the crowd so you're crushed sideways and you're still able to breathe.
- Don't follow the crowd, try to get to places where there is a physical barrier between you and the other people, such as a building.
- If you're stuck, assume a boxer stance to avoid being pushed over by the crowd. Keep both feet spread apart, one foot ahead of the other, arms around your chest area, knees bent lightly, and shuffle your feet when the crowd moves.

How to Survive an Active Shooter

Before leaving on my first trip to Israel, my friend Catherine warned me to hit the deck if I hear gunshots, then look to see where the sounds originated. Instead of looking to where the sounds were coming from, then hit the floor once you realize it's something dangerous like a shootout. It didn't make much sense to me at the time.

Until I arrived in Tel Aviv my first night and a few friends picked me up and took me out to eat a pizza. I had only been in the country for about two hours, and as I raised a slice of pizza to my mouth, we heard a loud boom. Everyone in the restaurant immediately hit the deck. I, on the other hand, caught myself looking around, confused, looking for the source of the sound.

My friends shouted at me to drop to the ground, so I dropped after a few moments, and waited for cues on what to do next. As I lay there, I remembered that everyone in Israel has to serve in the military, the place I was in was full of young people who were either in the military or just served their mandatory service, and shootings were frequent in Israel at this time. Every one of my five friends had recently served in the military, so these folks knew what to do.

After a few moments, everyone got up and cleared out, and I started collecting the pizza to carry out with me and eat. That was the second mistake my friends pointed out as they just left their belongings behind. By carrying out the pizza box, I just made myself a more significant and noticeable target for a shooter to focus on when shooting into a crowd. I would also be less mobile if I had to run away if the shooter were to approach us quickly.

If you hear gunshots or popping, stay calm, and stay focused. Remember, there could be more than one shooter. Use these suggestions to help you plan a strategy for survival.

Assume they are gunshots and don't investigate. Decide one of three courses of action:

- Can you stay where you are and secure yourself from the shooter? If so, secure yourself, and call 911.
- Can you escape, hide, or get secure from the shooter? Get to a safe place and call 911.
- Are you able to get away or not? If you're unable to escape, either shield yourself or prepare to take aggressive action to protect yourself.

Deciding on the best course of action

- If an active shooter is outside your building, go to a room that can be locked, close and lock all the windows and doors, turn off all the lights, get everyone down on the floor, make sure that no one is visible from outside, and call 911. Do not respond to unfamiliar voices. It could be the shooter attempting to lure victims out. Do not respond to any voice commands until you can verify it is a police officer.

- If an active shooter is in the same building as you, follow the directions from the previous paragraph. If your room cannot be locked, barricade the door with heavy furniture such as desks, tables, and bookcases. If possible, exit the building, run, alert others not to enter, as you exit the area/building.
- If an active shooter enters where you are, remain calm, and call 911. If you can't speak, leave the line open so the dispatcher can listen to what's happening. Sometimes the location of a 911 call can be determined without talking. If you can't escape or hide, shield yourself (desk, book bags, computers, etc.). Try to negotiate with the shooter.
- If you and others decide to overpower the shooter, know this will be risky and cannot be done half-heartedly. Spread out and don't stand in a group. You may be able to disorient the shooter by yelling and throwing items. When the shooter leaves the area, go to a safe place, and do not touch anything that was around the shooter. The police will need to investigate afterward, and you don't want to disturb clues.

Plan an Escape Route

If you decide to flee an active shooting situation, make sure you have an escape route, and plan in mind.

- Don't carry anything while fleeing. Move fast, stay calm, keep your hands visible, and follow the instructions of any police officer.
- The police officer's verbal commands will be loud and insistent.
- Do not ask questions, but provide critical information you might have (such as the location of the shooter).
- Do not remove injured people, leave wounded victims where they are, and notify authorities of their location as soon as possible.
- Do not leave the area until advised it is safe to do so

by police. Police will want to question all witnesses.

How to Escape a Kidnapping Attempt

- Kidnappers scope out tourist areas, so try to blend in as much as possible. Don't wear flashy accessories or clothing, and don't use ATMs that are facing the street.
- Try to avoid taking a taxi, instead use public transportation or walk.
- If you're driving, keep at least one car space of distance between you and the car ahead of you. Kidnappers will try to box you in with other vehicles. If you leave space, you'll be able to escape. Kidnappers will also try to enter your car, so keep your windows up and your doors locked.
- If you sense danger, call 911 or the equivalent, and leave your phone in speaker mode and place it in your pocket so the emergency services personnel can hear what's happening.
- Grab your keys and hold them between your fingers and get ready to punch and puncture the attacker's face. Do as much damage as you can. Assume the worst and act as if your life depended on it: kick, scream, bite, scratch, yell for help, draw attention, and fight dirty.
- If you're overwhelmed or they're about to kill you, then save your energy for the next chance to fight or escape.
- If they try to tie your hands, present your hands in front of you. Spread your fingers and your legs, so you create space, or the restraints won't be loose enough for you to escape later.
- If you're blindfolded or placed in a trunk, try to remember as much information as you can, such as nearby landmarks, the direction your vehicle is moving, smells, and sounds such as trains, flowing water, animals. When you escape later, you'll be able to use this information to tell rescuers where to find you.

Taxi

To avoid being kidnapped or having your items stolen in a taxi, always place your bags in your lap and on the seat next to you. When you arrive, open the door, put your bags on the ground on the side of the car, then step out of the taxi to pay the driver. If you have someone with you, as a spouse, have them do the same on the opposite side of the car, so you're both stepping out at the same time. If you step out and wait for the second person to get out, you risk the taxi driving off with your partner, extorting them or holding them for ransom, etc. If you don't have room and have to place them in the trunk, then have the driver get off to open and unload your bags for you.

Uber or Lyft is much safer than taxis anywhere in the world since the drivers are pre-vetted, and if you forget something in the vehicle, you can contact them through the application and recover your belongings. It also helps you avoid price gouging.

In some countries, riding a taxi can be dangerous, so if you have to take a taxi, it's best to have your hotel order you one. Having the hotel order you a cab may be more expensive, but you will most likely get someone who is vetted and wants to continue to receive business from the hotel. They will treat you well and make sure they don't damage their relationship with the hotel.

Hiding Places for Money

Bras with removable pads and tampon tubes are good places to hide money. People tend to stay away from personal items when they search or steal from you. Other items include: money belt, hollow bottom shaving cream bottles, the lining of your hat, under the pad in your shoe, between your smartphone cover and your phone, or a scarf with a hidden wallet.

Traveling with Expensive Equipment

If you have cameras, laptops, etc., use kids backpacks

or diaper bags to carry them. No one will think of stealing them. The fancy bags attract attention and advertise that you have something expensive in there.

Make your luggage look specific. Tie colored bands to it or stick stickers on your bags, so you can spot your luggage easily. As a backup, take pictures of your luggage and your items so you can show the images to someone in case you lose them.

False Wallet

Ideally, you should use a money pouch to hide your money. But if you prefer a wallet, try the following tricks:

- Wrap your wallet with a rubber band so you can feel if someone is trying to pull it out of your pocket. The rubber band will twist in your pocket, sending a vibration through your clothing, and let you know someone has their hand in your pocket.
- Carry it sideways instead of up and down. That makes it harder to pull out your wallet.
- Use this wallet for daily expenses in case you get robbed.

Security

Don't use the door hanger that says, "Please Make Up Room." This lets people know you're not in your room and invites them to try to break in while you're out. Instead, place the "Do Not Disturb" sign to keep people away.

Make sure you and those traveling with you have pictures of each other in case one of you gets lost.

Hide cameras and don't read maps out in the open this makes it obvious you don't know where you're going, and you'll attract unwanted attention. Read them in restaurants or bathrooms to avoid unwanted attention.

Women Travelers

Follow the same general precautions, but be extra

sensitive to local female customs and make sure you are observing them. Keep in mind that most of the world has different social norms for men and women. The world has many different customs and cultures. Take the time to understand and learn from other cultures, and don't try to force your ideas on others. Enjoy yourself, this is not the time to make a stand for social justice.

Remember that a single woman traveling alone is not the norm, so you're always going to attract more attention. Even still, the travel trails are full of single female travelers, but they tend to be smarter than their male counterparts and avoid problems.

Avoid attracting attention and blend in as much as possible; buy some local loose clothing to avoid unwanted attention. Dress conservatively and don't wear too much make-up. Wear glasses to avoid making eye contact with people and possibly giving the impression that you're looking for company.   Be open to spending a little more to stay in better areas, pay for Uber or use public transportation rather than walking the streets at night, and stay out of lonely places. Don't drink too much or do drugs which will make you an easy target.

Check-in regularly with family and friends. Be more selective as to whom you hang out with and try to group up with other travelers for outings to night spots or tourist attractions as there is always strength in numbers.

The Middle East, Asia, and Africa are regions where women have to be more conscious about what they're doing to avoid issues. Overall, your biggest worry is going to be fending off local men, so have fun, but be alert.

Avoid Offending

Wherever you go, observe the locals and do as they do. Pay attention to gender-specific behavior, learn the local customs, and always be respectful. If the locals are removing their shoes before entering a building, wearing headscarves, bowing their heads when they greet each other, kneeling before entering temples, etc., do precisely the same and you'll earn a lot of respect from them. Avoid unwanted attention for disrespecting or offending, and generally just be smart. If you have different cultural or religious beliefs that you practice at home, that's great, but for now, you're in someone else's world, so forget your ego and fall in line.

I traveled with some friends who refused to go into churches in Mexico because they didn't believe in Jesus, and when we checked into our hotel, they would ask permission to remove or cover religious decorations in their rooms. They missed out on seeing some of the best tourist sites, offended people in the hotels when they would ask to have statues of the Virgin Mary removed from their rooms, and generally stressed themselves out walking around thinking about how they needed to avoid these things. We cannot change the outside world, we can only change our attitudes towards it. Respect other people's way of life, by not imposing your beliefs on them.

When you communicate with people, smile and use a soft, low toned voice. Be polite, learn basic local phrases such as thank you, excuse me, and I'm sorry. This will take you a long way anywhere you go. If you make a mistake, smile and excuse yourself. People are more likely to forgive a foreigner if you smile.

When it comes to tipping, ask around what is customary, and follow the locals' lead.

Don't take photos of sensitive military areas, religious practices, demonstrations, or political places without prior permission. Ask permission before taking photos. Be cool. You represent yourself, your family, and your country. Wherever you go, always be respectful. You don't want to ruin it for the next traveler.

Changing Money

Use pre-booked online money changers or go to high-end hotels. They tend to have the best exchange rates.

ATM Cards

Although withdrawing from an ATM carries charges, most of the time getting the best exchange rate offered offsets these charges. Make each withdrawal large, so you can cut down on the frequency of charges incurred. You usually get charged two fees, one from the host bank and one from your bank, for each withdrawal. Setting up a bank account with an online bank, such as Simple, will help you avoid ATM fees altogether.

Credit Cards

Use a credit card for all your purchases; credit cards will give you the best exchange rate offered that month. Just make sure it's a travel card that doesn't charge the 3% foreign transaction fee. While you're at it, get a credit card with the best travel rewards programs.

Don't use your credit card for a cash advance, the fees and interest rates are much higher. The interest rates on cash advances also begin immediately instead of having the 30-day grace period.

If the merchant requests to charge your card in U.S. dollars instead of the local currency, decline it. When paying with your credit card, always pay in the local currency. This is a trick called dynamic currency conversion. The exchange rate is usually the worst, and the merchant can add fees on top of that. Make your charges in the original currency and let your credit card company figure out the exchange rate.

Wire Transfers

While on a trip to the Galapagos Islands, I ran out of US dollars, and the locals prefer cash payments for tours and excursions. The bank fees are unusually high, and the locals can charge you up to 15% more if you use a credit card, which they say covers their bank fees. I needed $1000; if I paid with a credit card, it would cost me $150 upfront to the merchant plus whatever fees my bank charged, or if I used Western Union, it was only $18 in fees. A promotion was running when I needed the money, so I sent myself cash for free, and I could pick it up in about 30 minutes at any Western Union. If you need money in an emergency, consider using the Western Union application to send yourself cash

Street Currency Exchangers

In some countries, the only way to exchange money is through people who engage in the informal practice of trading currencies in public places. Street money changers can be commonly found in tourist areas, marketplaces, transportation hubs, and other locations with high foot traffic. While they provide a convenient option for currency exchange, it's essential to exercise caution when dealing with street money changers, as the rates they offer may only sometimes be competitive. There can be risks associated with informal currency exchange services. It's advisable to compare rates with authorized currency exchange offices or banks to ensure you get the best value for your money and to be aware of potential scams or counterfeit currency issues when using street money changers. I've had counterfeit currency given to me in Costa Rica, Colombia, etc...

Chapter 16.

Travel Health

Body Building Expo Los Angeles California

These are generally recommended guidelines for traveling. Prepare yourself medically before a trip by having a pre-travel examination with your health professional. Most folks exert themselves more than usual during a trip. It's recommended that you check your health before leaving, so you don't have any surprises or have to deal with unknown health issues while you're far away from home. For 19-39-year-olds, have a physical every 2-3 years. After 40, checkups should include an eye exam, blood pressure, head, neck, heart, abdomen, peripheral pulses, reflexes, and nervous system. Women should have a Pap smear, and both men and women should have rectal exams.

- Routine blood tests should include cholesterol, urine, and blood sugar test. Stool tests are done as needed.
- Colonoscopy should be done every 5-10 years for people over 50, and if you ever see blood in your stools.
- ECG is recommended for people over 45 years old.
- A chest X-ray is done depending on past medical history of tuberculosis and/or smoking.
- Mammograms should be done every 1-2 years for women over 40. Yearly for women who have a history of cancer in the family.
- Medical exams after a trip are not necessary unless you have symptoms of fever, jaundice, diarrhea, skin disorders, genital disorders, or persistent cough. All of these may be caused by a variety of ailments, including malaria, tuberculosis, filariasis, hepatitis, typhoid, parasites, typhus, trachoma, trypanosomiasis, and sexually transmitted diseases.
- Early detection and treatment of these disorders can prevent long-term complications.

The International Certificate of Vaccination

Official documentation is used as proof of vaccination against a disease when there's a requirement to enter a country. Carry a hardcopy with you and keep digital copies online, to avoid being denied entry into countries that require it.

Diarrhea

Wherever you live on the planet, your body has a symbiotic relationship with the microorganisms around you. You need bacteria to digest food and keep your body healthy. If you eat locally grown food, your body has a specific set of bacteria to help break it down. That's why diarrhea is common when you travel, because you have to grow the bacteria to break down the food you're eating in the new surroundings.

Any time you travel, you're at a higher risk of getting sick, because your body is not used to the microorganisms and food in the environment that you're visiting. Once you go to another city, even within the same country, you're going to be interacting biologically with an entirely new environment, which is going to include even more varieties of microorganisms if you go to another country with different sanitation standards, foods, and climate. If you travel from a developed country, like the USA, to a developing country, it increases substantially the probability of you becoming ill, because you live in a place that is generally cleaner. The cleaner the environment you live in, the weaker and more susceptible you'll be in these new environments.

Your body becomes stressed when you move to new environments. Your GED, sleeping patterns are altered, maybe you got diarrhea from the new foods you're eating, you're rushing around sightseeing, and perhaps exerting yourself more than you normally would. Diarrhea is the most common travel health disorder that affects about 80% of travelers. Symptoms are loose, watery bowel movements. Diarrhea is present when you have three or more loose stools in one day.

Diarrhea treatments include eating raw green bananas or raw potatoes, charcoal tablets, Kaopectate, Kaolin, and Pepto-Bismol. Lomotil and Imodium are strong antidiarrheal medications and can provide immediate relief, but should not be used if you have blood in your stools or fever. They should be discontinued after 48 hours of use. Drink plenty of water, and add oral rehydration packets to avoid dehydration caused by diarrhea.

Travelers with severe symptoms of diarrhea, as in three or more loose stools in eight hours, can be prescribed an antibiotic treatment such as Bactrim, Ciprobay, Lexinor, or Vibramycin. If you have a history of having a loose stomach, fill a prescription with one of these treatments and carry it with you in case the country where you're traveling requires a prescription. Vibramycin, aka Doxycycline, should not be taken by pregnant women or children under ten years old. As always, a doctor should be consulted if symptoms persist.

If you have access to a doctor, that's always your best option. This ensures you don't take the wrong medication or build resistance to bacteria due to improper antibiotic use. These antibiotics are recommended if you know you're going somewhere where doctors are hard to get hold of.

Vaccinations

Vaccinations, in my opinion, are an excellent investment, especially if you're going to be traveling. Danger has to be measured by the probability of that danger actually happening. Whenever possible, it's best to take steps to lower the likelihood of something happening to you. For example, wearing a seat belt will increase your chances of surviving a car accident by 80%. It doesn't mean it's 100%, or that there are any guarantees you won't get hurt wearing one, but it will increase your chances of survival.

Vaccines lower your risks of getting sick. I've had several friends over the years who became extremely ill or died in other countries. I've also had patients come to the hospital where I work who had contracted illnesses in other countries and suffered unnecessarily due to inadequate preparation. Don't put yourself in this type of situation if you can avoid it. A vaccine is one of your first lines of defense, the easiest and most cost-effective.

Check out the CDC website, which has the best available information anywhere. It has the most comprehensive information on how to prepare to visit any place on the planet. It has every country organized from A to Z, so you can just click on the country and get information on how to prepare to visit that location. It includes travel warnings and emergencies happening in that region, recommended vaccines and medications, a safe and healthy travel section, a healthy travel packing list, travel health notices, and what to do after your trip if you're not feeling well.

Malaria

Malaria is the second most common infectious disease leading to death in the world, after tuberculosis. It's a mosquito-borne infectious disease, caused by a plasmodium parasite. The severity depends on the species of plasmodium you're infected with. Malaria causes symptoms that typically include fever, chills, tiredness, vomiting, and headaches. You usually start feeling the symptoms a week to four weeks after you've been infected.

My friend Don Reddington contracted malaria while traveling. He's had it for over fifty years and has occasional fevers as a result of the lifelong infection, but it hasn't stopped him from traveling into his 80s. If you're able to survive malaria like Don, then it's a good story to share. If you don't, then you don't, and those are the people you don't hear from. Don't go by uninformed overgeneralizations from others; do your research and be prepared.

You can look up free malaria maps online to find out if you need to take precautions. If you're traveling to areas where malaria is prevalent, you can take protective drugs before, during, and after the trip. Treatment includes antimalarial drugs.

Some people prefer to use potent mosquito repellent (30% DEET or higher) at all times, and spray their clothes with Permethrin. Permethrin is a pesticide that can be sprayed on shoes, socks, bags, and clothes, and it lasts for several weeks, even after being washed. It's excellent for protection from ticks, mosquitoes, lice, scabies, and other parasites.

Jet Lag

Also known as desynchronosis, jet lag is a sleep disorder that can affect those who travel quickly across multiple time zones. It happens when the body's internal clock is out of sync with the new environment. When environmental factors such as light exposure, mealtimes, and rest times change, your body has to adapt. Symptoms are fatigue, insomnia, difficulty concentrating, and irregular eating patterns. Jet lag tends to get worse as you age; it takes longer to recover from the exertion of the journey, because your body is weaker.

Eleven Ways to Decrease Jet Lag

1. Prepare for your trip while still at home. A few days before departure, try going to sleep and waking up at the same time you would be doing in the new time zone. For example, if you have a two-hour time difference east of where you live, try to go to sleep a couple of hours earlier than usual. If you're going west, stay awake two extra hours.

If you have a history of problems with jet lag, then avoid overnight flights. These flights cause more issues as you arrive in the morning tired, and then you have to start your day. On the other hand, arriving in the afternoon or evening is a much better option since you only have to stay awake for a few hours; you get to explore for a little while, have dinner, and then go to bed.

2. Prepare yourself mentally; once you board the plane, set your watch to the new destination's local time. Sleep and stay awake on the flight as if you were in your new location, regardless if it's still daytime or night time on the flight.

3. Be prepared to stay awake or sleep in the plane so you can follow the sleeping schedule in the destination's time zone. If you know you're going to have to sleep on the flight, especially during daylight hours, wear comfortable clothes, pack a neck cushion, earplugs, and a sleep mask. Once you board the plane, if you see empty seats, ask for a row to yourself so you can lie down horizontally and sleep more comfortably. If you have to stay awake, then watch movies or bring a good book to read.

4. Melatonin is a hormone produced by your body to

help you sleep. Melatonin works with your body's circadian rhythm to regulate your sleep-wake cycle. Melatonin levels increase in your body as it gets dark outside, telling your body that it's time to sleep. Take 0.5 mg of melatonin to help you sleep and adjust to jet lag.

5. Choose foods to help you stay on your sleep schedule. Protein-rich foods such as beef, fish, or eggs will help you stay awake, whereas carbohydrate-rich foods such as rice, potatoes, pasta, or overeating will make you sleepy.

6. Pressurized cabins on planes have low humidity, which causes moisture to evaporate from the body and may result in dehydration. The dry air can also cause the cilia in the throat to become less active at sweeping out viruses and bacteria, so you become more susceptible to illness. Stay hydrated with water and juice throughout the flight. Avoid alcohol and caffeine as their adverse effects, including dehydration, are multiplied while you're at a high altitude. Having wine to help you sleep has limited effectiveness, and it will dehydrate you and make it harder for you to adjust to the new time zone. Coffee and black tea can also dehydrate you and should be avoided. Bring your refillable bottle so you can have it filled up with water or juice when drinks are served to help you prevent dehydration and reduce the trash you create.

Eat something salty before flying to help you retain more water in your body during a flight.

7. If you're flying a long distance, schedule a layover for at least one night along your route. This will reduce jet lag and give you an opportunity to see an additional location.

8. As soon as you arrive at your destination, follow the circadian rhythm of the location. Don't sleep during the day even if you're tired; wait till the evening. Sunlight inhibits the production of melatonin, the hormone in your body that makes you feel tired so you can sleep. If it's daytime, go outside, this will help your body adapt to the new environment.

9. Give your body a few days to adjust to the new environment. Flights can tire you out and cause fatigue. It's best to start slow and allow your body to rest and recover in the new environment and time zone.

10. Exercise before, during, and after you arrive at your location to help reset your circadian rhythms to normal. Exercise will help alleviate disruptions to your body clock. While on your flight during awake times, get up and walk at least once per hour, complete squats by the restrooms, and contract and relax your leg and butt muscles while in your seat to get the blood pumping.

11. Use the same strategies on your flight back home to avoid jet lag at the end of your trip.

Nausea

Nausea is a queasy sensation, including an urge to vomit. Nausea can have causes that aren't due to underlying disease. Examples include motion from a car, boat, or plane, taking pills on an empty stomach, eating too much or too little, or drinking too much alcohol. Focusing the eyes on objects straight ahead may help. Avoid overeating, alcohol, and smoking before travel. Oral or patch medications can prevent or treat symptoms.

One effective alternative treatment is taking a smell of the essential oil peppermint when you're feeling nauseous.

Seasonal Affective Disorder

Also known as SAD, is a mood disorder characterized by depression that occurs at the same time every year. SAD usually happens during the winter months.

One winter, I flew to Switzerland to visit my girlfriend and experienced my first ever blizzard. We ended up spending several days indoors due to the weather, and I started feeling really down. I remember calling my mom and spending a long time talking to her and the rest of my family. I just didn't want to get off the phone. I even started crying at one point and telling my mom how depressed I was. Being from sunny Southern California, I had never experienced snow storms. Understanding how weather can affect your psychological state will help you deal with temporary feelings of depression and help you realize when it's time for a change. I ended up boarding a plane to sunny Italy, and all of my sad feelings disappeared.

Vacation Romance

My good friend Mike often tells me about a girl he met over 40 years ago while backpacking in Australia. He had planned to travel there for three weeks alone but met a beautiful girl from England and ended up canceling all of his tours and activities to spend the rest of their vacation together. When they both ran out of money, they started working as field workers, saved money to buy a motorcycle, and traveled the country for nine more months.

On their last day in Sydney, Mike and Laura tearfully promised to keep in touch and clung to each other until the airline staff threatened to leave. Saying good-bye was sad, but shortly after, the situation's reality became apparent. The lovers started to face obstacles such as careers, another time zone, friends, family, and wondering if it could ever work out.

Although they meant to see each other again, things never seemed to work out. Mike has always remembered Laura and wondered what if? Most of us who travel can relate as we've met the most amazing people at the right time and in the right place, and it seemed like something out of a fairy tale. The fun, the drinks, the adventure all made everything even more memorable. These travel experiences can be amongst the most fulfilling and life-altering. The romantic memories can stay with you for a lifetime and remind you of a moment in time when you felt absolute bliss.

A holiday romance is usually temporary or a casual relation between two strangers that develops profoundly in a short space of time. Sharing one of the best times of your life with someone can make it challenging to let go or part ways. If you have reasons why it's not best to hold on to the relationship, here are five tips for letting go.

1. Understand that your relationship existed in an unusual setting. Without your attention on work, family, school, or anything else happening in your life. You're able to be consumed by the excitement and novelty of the new setting without having to be concerned about the consequences.

2. Don't try to stay in touch with your vacation romance. A relationship that intense needs to stop as suddenly as it started. Once you get back into your routine, you'll get back into a stable emotional position. Try to avoid focusing on the good points they chose to spotlight about themselves, or you'll miss them more.

3. Stay busy with your friends and family doing things you enjoy. Share your feelings with your confidants to ease heartache or loneliness.

4. Focus on your work. After a nice vacation, your mind will be clear, and it'll be an ideal time to channel that pent-up energy into a productive outlet.

5. Remember the beautiful experience, appreciate it for what it was, and make peace with its ending. Don't try and rationalize all the reasons you two were meant to be or could have worked things out. Instead, look forward to your next trip and all the exciting people you'll meet on that one.

Culture Shock

Although not very common, it's a feeling of disorientation when someone suddenly experiences an unfamiliar culture and a way of life that is different from one's own. It causes short term feelings of frustration, which usually goes away the more you immerse yourself into the new culture.

The Harmful Effects of Heat

Avoid excessive sun exposure and drink extra fluids when traveling in warmer climates to avoid dehydration. Dehydration can cause irritability, constipation, headaches, lower your blood pressure, cramping, and fatigue. Dehydration is the number one reason for hospital visits.

Heat exhaustion is the body's response to loss of water and salt through excessive sweating. If heat exhaustion is left untreated, it can lead to heat stroke, which can have long-term health effects.

A heat rash occurs when sweat ducts get clogged and trap perspiration under the skin. Sunburn is a result of excessive exposure to the sun's ultraviolet rays.

To protect yourself from heat, wear light-weight clothing, stay hydrated, and avoid strenuous activity. The skin needs to be moisturized to prevent dry or flaky skin. Within ten minutes of bathing, apply body lotion help retain moisture in the skin. Water-based moisturizers are recommended for hot weather because they are typically lighter weight than oil-based moisturizers. Sunscreen of SPF 30 or higher is ideal for most people year-round.

Electrolytes

Electrolytes in the human body are a combination of body fluids and minerals. This mixture allows for electrically charged particles (ions) in the body to carry the electrical energy necessary for many functions, including muscle contractions and transmission of nerve impulses. When your body is deficient in electrolytes, you'll experience dehydration whose symptoms include muscle cramps, headache, dizziness, or fatigue.

To help prevent dehydration, you can make yourself an electrolyte drink anywhere in the world. All you need is something with sugar, water and salt in it. An easy recipe to remember is ¼ cup of fruit juice, ¼ teaspoon of salt, and ¾ cup of water. If available, drink coconut water with ¼ teaspoon of salt, or even plain, as it's a natural electrolyte drink.

How Much Water to Drink?

The minimum amount of water you should drink is eight glasses a day. However, you can still become dehydrated and suffer health effects from drinking eight glasses of water.

One year, I traveled to Egypt in July, and the temperature reached 122 degrees Fahrenheit, the hottest and driest weather I had ever experienced in my life. At first, I was surprised to see how few tourists were visiting the pyramids until I realized how difficult it was to travel under such hot and dry conditions. I had to carry three 1.5-liter bottles of water in my backpack at all times. Whenever I was talking to someone, I had to take a drink of water before I started speaking and before I could finish the sentence, because my mouth would become incredibly dry. It felt as if someone was shoving hot cotton in my mouth when the scorching air entered my mouth. I noticed that I was barely going to the restroom, as I lost most fluids through my mouth when I spoke in the hot air and from all the sweating, I was doing to keep my body temperature stable.

At home, I'm running marathons, wrestling, and involved in multiple sports. At times I exercise up to eight hours a day. However, in this hot climate I only walked or used public transportation as much as possible to avoid the sun.

I ended up staying inside during the hottest parts of the day and still averaged twelve 1.5-liter bottles of water a day. That adds up to forty-eight glasses of water, just to feel comfortable and carry on normal daily activities. So, don't limit yourself to eight glasses of water. The amount of water you need is going to depend on the climate you're visiting versus the climate you're accustomed to, and your health, activity level, and conditioning.

As a general rule, drink water whenever you feel thirsty. Your body will let you know when you're thirsty. Don't ignore the feeling of thirst or it will go away, and you'll drink even less water, which will only put you at a higher risk for heat related problems.

The Harmful Effects of Cold

Frostbite is caused by cold temperature damaging tissues of your body, usually your ears, nose, cheeks, chin, fingers, and toes. Frostbitten skin will feel numb and look white or gray. Frostbite is not painful; you won't notice as it sets in slowly and causes tissue damage. When it's freezing, you have to keep pinching your nose and cheeks to make sure there's still feeling left.

On below freezing days, don't wash your face in the morning, so you don't remove the natural oil produced by your skin and lose the protection from cold weather it provides.

Hypothermia occurs when you're exposed to cold weather for a prolonged period of time, and your body temperature drops below 95°F (35°C) and loses more heat than it can make. Hypothermia causes shivering, clumsiness, confusion, tiredness, or urinating more than usual. If not treated quickly, hypothermia can be deadly.

Being exposed to cold weather for prolonged periods of time can cause a heart attack. Because it causes your heart to work harder than usual to keep you warm, which increases your heart rate and blood pressure.

Beware of prolonged exposure to cold weather, wear warm clothing, and if you're still cold, seek shelter somewhere warmer.

Hepatitis A & B

Hepatitis A and B are the two most common types of viral hepatitis. Other types of hepatitis are C, D, and E. Hepatitis is a viral infection that attacks the liver. There are vaccinations available for Hep A and B that are strongly recommended. You can contract hepatitis through contact with blood and bodily fluids.

First Aid

If you don't have basic knowledge of first aid, then pick up a copy of the Red Cross First Aid Manual and learn the basics of how to treat sprains and strains, cuts and skin abrasions, burns, CPR and the ABC's (Airway, Breathing, Compressions), and how to treat choking victims.

How to Find Doctors When You Need Them

- Hotel doctors: Many will visit you in your room.
- Embassy referrals: Many will speak your language.
- Travel information organizations such as travel agencies.
- International travel assistance: A list of doctors is usually provided by your travel health insurance company, or you can contact them and they'll recommend doctors close to you.

Blood Transfusions

Risks of blood transfusions: allergic reactions, infectious disease, the transmission of drugs, and bacterial contamination. The safest blood to use is your own. It can be stored for up to ten years. Try to avoid blood transfusions in foreign countries at all cost. For more severe blood loss, you can take plasma expanders to help increase vessel volume until a safer blood source is available.

Antibiotics

Antibiotics have extended our lives by about ten years since being introduced in the 1940s. Antibiotics will not cure viral infections, only bacterial infections. Take antibiotics only when needed, or you'll build up a resistance to them, and they won't help you when you really need them. If you take antibiotics, make sure you complete the entire course. Not finishing your antibiotics can cause new drug-resistant strains of the bacteria, causing you more problems. Recognize antibiotic side effects such as rash, diarrhea, vomiting, abdominal pain, and nausea.

Sometimes taking antibiotics can cause diarrhea, because it wipes out both the good and the bad bacteria, which causes a lack of good bacteria that help digest food properly. In some cases, harmful bacteria, like Clostridium difficile (C diff), may overgrow and cause infections, so avoid overdosing and taking unnecessary antibiotics.

Other Medications

Other medications commonly used during traveling: Aspirin, Ibuprofen, Naproxen, and other non-steroidal anti-inflammatory drugs. These medications are used to relieve pain, while aspirin is usually taken to reduce fever. Only take as directed and do not take on an empty stomach as this can cause stomach lining irritation, gastritis, or even an ulcer.

- Paracetamol and acetaminophen are commonly used to relieve pain and fever. Unlike aspirin, they do not irritate the stomach, but taking excessive amounts can cause damage to the liver.
- Antihistamines and decongestants are commonly used to relieve the symptoms of colds, cases of flu, and upper respiratory illnesses. Antihistamines have a sedating effect, and it's best to avoid driving and using heavy equipment. Decongestants work by decreasing swelling and inflammation, allowing air to flow through and drain the nose.
- A tube of antibiotic cream is good for cuts and scrapes, which can easily become infected.
- If you have a history of constipation, laxatives may help.
- A daily multivitamin is useful in case your diet is unbalanced.
- For motion sickness, bring Dramamine.
- Follow the directions on the medications you're taking. Some of them have to be taken with food, so be aware.
- Be aware of how drugs mix. You can have serious

side effects by mixing drugs.

- Be aware of which drugs should not be taken by pregnant women and children.

Travel Exercise Program

There are literally thousands of workout programs you can find on the web and stream live on YouTube for ideas to use in your room. Here's a sample of what I use in the mornings to keep me in shape when I travel. Use the peripheral heart action workouts, where you alternate one upper body exercise and one lower body exercise. By alternating upper and lower body exercise, you cause the blood to flow back and forth creating more work for your heart.

Start by pairing one upper body exercise with one lower body exercise.

- Sample exercise plan:
- Push up/jump squats
- Diamond push up/lunges
- Plank/toe raises
- Spider crawl/bear crawl

Do one set of 6-8 repetitions of the upper body exercise, then rest, not more than 10 seconds, before starting one set of the lower body exercise of 6-8 repetitions. Take a 90 second rest before starting the next pair. Then repeat the pair of exercises 3 times, until switching to the next pair of exercises.

Airplane Seat Exercises

1. Leg lifts: Sit on your seat. Close your feet. Now pull your knees up and down without touching the floor with your feet. Complete one set of 10 repetitions every hour that you're on the plane.

2. Exaggerated neck roll: Relax your shoulders and drop them down your back, so your spine is elongated. Tilt your head to the right and roll it back and to the left. Reverse.

Complete one set of 5 repetitions in each direction every hour that you're on the plane.

3. Knee circles: Sitting on your seat, lift your knees like in the previous exercise and do circles without your feet touching the floor. Complete one set of 10 repetitions every hour that you're on the plane. Repeat circling your knees in the opposite direction.

4. High knees: Bend forward slightly, and put your hands around one of your knees. Then slowly pull the knee towards your chest. Hold for 10 seconds and then alternate knees. Complete one set of 5 repetitions every hour that you're on the plane.

5. Crossover lift: as you are sitting, place the ankle of your left leg on top of your right leg. Now push your right leg up and down. Complete one set of 10 repetitions every hour that you're on the plane. Then repeat after switching legs.

6. Upper body twists: from a seated position, sit straight up in your seat and rest your forearms on the armrest. Then twist your torso, so you're facing the left side of the plane without actually moving your head. Keep your feet planted on the floor and hold this position for five seconds while practicing deep breaths. Then slowly twist to the opposite side for five more breaths. Complete one set of 5 repetitions every hour that you're on the plane.

7. Stand on fists: make fists with your hands and place them next to you close to your knees. Push your weight forward, and then pull yourself up. Your feet are off the ground, and your butt is off the seat. Hold this position for 20 seconds. Complete one every hour that you're on the plane.

8. Stand on fists pulses: Same as the previous exercise, except you lift yourself and start doing pulses (quick lifts) with your knees.

9. Tricep lifts: Place your hand on the bars of your seat. Ask your neighbor's permission and point your elbows point toward the back instead of outwards. Now lift yourself up

and down using your triceps. Your feet should touch the floor for balance, but don't use them to help yourself get up. Complete one set of 10 repetitions every hour that you're on the plane.

10. Harder tricep lift: get in the same position as before, but lift your feet off the ground this time. Complete one set of 10 repetitions every hour that you're on the plane.

11. Walking lunges: This exercise is optional if you complete the rest of the suggested activities. A good option if the other tasks are just not meeting your needs, and you need more movement. Once the aisle is clear, the fasten seatbelt sign is off, stand up, count to ten, and start with both feet together. Take one step forward and lower your body towards the ground by bending your front leg. Move up by bringing the back leg forward to meet your front foot. Complete one set of 10 repetitions every hour that you're on the plane.

12. Calf raises: Hold onto a seat back or another sturdy object for support. Stand with your feet hip-distance apart and slowly rise onto your toes. Hold for a second or two, then slowly lower down. Complete one set of 10 repetitions every hour that you're on the plane.

13. Take a walk up the aisle: Do a full lap to the other end of the aircraft and then back to your seat. While you're up, shake out your arms and legs as well.

14. If you have limited mobility or are at high risk for blood clots. Compression socks are an excellent option to help increase blood flow and reduce swelling on long-haul flights.

Airplane Seated Stretches

Here is a stretch protocol to be implemented while in your airplane seat to prevent health problems related to sitting for long periods of time. The same stretches are useful in just about any situation.

Airplane Stretches

Photocopy this page and take it along on your next flight. Stretching on the plane will relieve stress and stiffness and allow you to arrive in a more relaxed state. Don't be surprised if your fellow passengers follow your example and start stretching too. Especially good to do just before you land.

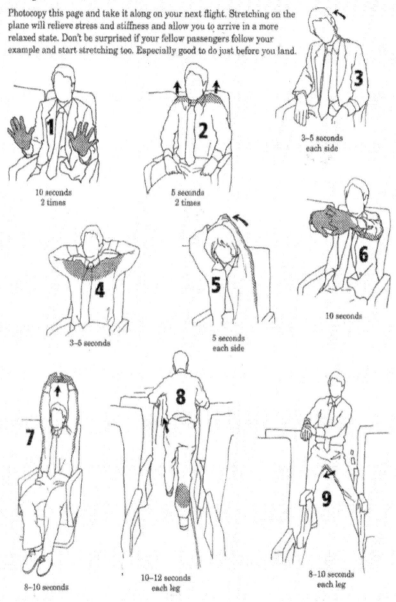

1
10 seconds
2 times

2
5 seconds
2 times

3
3–5 seconds
each side

4
3–5 seconds

5
5 seconds
each side

6
10 seconds

7
8–10 seconds

8
10–12 seconds
each leg

9
8–10 seconds
each leg

Chapter 17.

How to Travel the World in a
Wheelchair or on Crutches

Sleeping in a Teepee Coos Bay Oregon

Traveling requires special planning and preparation if
you're in a wheelchair or on crutches. The complexity of
your trip will grow depending on your level of disability. By
understanding the variables that could slow your journey,
you can plan accordingly to overcome them.

If you've recently had surgery, speak to your doctor
regarding travel restrictions. Typically, after surgery, you're
at higher risk for blood clots for up to six months, and

165

plane travel increases the risk even more. When scheduling your flights, extend layovers between connecting flights to decrease the risk of blood clots. Keep in mind that the longer the trip, the higher the risk.

If your mobility is limited or you've recently had surgery, make sure you are moving your body every 1-2 hours for a few minutes to reduce the risk of blood clots. If you're able to stand supported, do toe raises. If you can't stand, then move your limbs while seated and complete isometric exercises. For example, press your hands together in a prayer position as hard as you can for ten seconds. You'll feel the tension in your chest and arms, yet your arms didn't move at all. For your legs, push your feet into the ground as hard as you can for ten seconds, so you'll feel the tension in your feet and legs. These are isometric exercises, where you have the static contraction of a muscle without any visible movement in the angle of the joint allowing your muscles to pump and circulate blood through the limb, which significantly reduces the risk of blood clots. Keep in mind to maintain your weight-bearing precautions if you have any. For example, if you're not supposed to put weight on your leg, don't stand on it; instead, use isometric exercises.

Before you start your trip, learn the rules so your trip will go smoother. The Americans with Disabilities Act covers people in the USA while on the ground, and the Air Carrier Access Act (ACAA) covers access on all flights to and from the US. Familiarizing yourself with the laws will help you understand what accommodations, facilities, and services should be available to you. It's a good idea to carry a copy with you in case you have issues with staff who may not be familiar with the accommodations they are required to provide you according to the law. If you have access-related questions, you can call the disability hotline operated by the US Department of Transportation at (800) 778-4838. If you have any pre-trip questions regarding the security screening process, contact the TSA at least 72 hours before your flight at (855) 787-2227.

Once you arrive at the airport, if you can't walk through

the metal detector unassisted, let the airport security or Transportation Security Administration (TSA) agent know. They will take you aside, hand-wand you, and give you a manual pat-down. Let the agents know if you have any sore or tender body parts before the screening. You also have the option for a private screening, if you prefer, with a companion of your choice present.

Wheelchair Accommodations

1. If you're not able to walk long distances, request an airport wheelchair when you make your reservation. If you plan on traveling with your wheelchair, let the airline know beforehand what type of an assistive device you have. Passengers with battery-powered wheelchairs have to arrive at the airport at least one hour before standard check-in time.

2. When making your plane reservations, request a seat with a flip-up armrest, which will make transfers much more manageable. A bulkhead is a divider that separates the classes or sections of a plane. These seats have extra legroom and are therefore easier to get in an out. Although not required by the ACAA, some airlines will routinely block bulkhead seats for passengers with limited mobility.

3. The ACAA also entitles you to stay in your wheelchair (if it has non-spillable batteries) until you get to the gate. Once you get to the gate, your wheelchair will be taken down to the cargo area, and you'll be transported to your seat in a high-back aisle chair if you can't walk. Once you get to your destination, your wheelchair or scooter will be delivered to you at the gate.

4. Bring assembly and disassembly instructions (in Spanish and English) for your mobility device with you to the airport. The ACAA requires that if a wheelchair or scooter is disassembled for transport, it must be returned to the passenger correctly assembled. Having assembly instructions available to the staff who'll be helping, you'll make things easier.

5. Planes that have more than one hundred seats have storage space aboard for one manual wheelchair. This space is available on a first-come basis, so try to get to the boarding area early.

6. Before you board the plane use the airport bathrooms, since they tend to be easier to access. Airplane bathrooms are small, and you need to be able to walk a few steps to use them. So have a backup plan such as wearing a diaper, in case you have an accident, it'll be easier to clean up.

7. Remember, many people are on crutches or wheelchairs, and airline staff have their protocols for helping such passengers. Ask for priority boarding and request special services staff to assist you.

8. Book hotels, tours, and trips to places that are wheelchair accessible. Pre-planning is vital, so you don't end up somewhere where wheelchair accessibility is not a consideration. If the location is not accessible and you have the funds, you can make the place convenient for you. By paying for private transportation and traveling with your wheelchair ramp, adaptive equipment, and a travel partner who can help you manage your equipment and help you access the location you're visiting. Check out Curb Free with Cory Lee for examples and strategies used by Cory Lee on how he travels the world in his power wheelchair.

Accommodations for Travelers with Crutches

If you're able to self-ambulate with crutches and partially weight bear, then you may be able to navigate most environments. However, airports may require long waits in lines for check-in or security clearance. Therefore, it's best to make arrangements with the airport before you arrive to have a wheelchair provided to you, to help you navigate the airport easier and decrease the risk of you falling due to fatigue.

1. Again you can request bulkhead seating. If you can afford the expense, upgrade to a higher-class seat, or ask to be seated next to empty seats, so you have more room to

navigate. The same goes for wheelchairs users.

2. Hotels in developed countries have a limited number of accessible rooms available. So, book rooms in advance so you can have a room with wider doorways and spacious bathrooms that make it easier for you to move around. Otherwise, most hotels have tub-shower combos, which are not accessible in a wheelchair and complicated when you're on crutches. Accessible rooms will usually provide a walk-in shower, grab bars, and a detachable showerhead.

3. Book hotels in advance and request rooms on the ground floor or near the elevator. If you'll need a wheelchair while on hotel grounds, reserve a wheelchair in advance with the hotel.

4. Make advanced preparations to see which airport shuttles and car rental buses can accommodate you. In developed countries, most transportation is fitted to support wheelchairs and folks with limited mobility on crutches.

5. Public transportation in developed countries typically have signs, symbols, and are wheelchair accessible.

6. Traveling will require you to expend more energy than you usually do in your everyday life. Therefore, it's best to train for your trip by spending more time walking on your crutches and/or wheeling yourself in your wheelchair.

7. If you can afford the expense, consider buying lighter mobility equipment for traveling. Items such as a lighter wheelchair, walker, lighter crutches, collapsible crutches, transport wheelchair, lighter cane, or a device that's easier to break down will make your trip easier.

8. Lighten your load as much as possible. Use luggage and materials that are lightweight, so you expend less energy moving your items. If possible, pack everything into one backpack, so it's less to keep track of and more comfortable for people who are helping you.

9. Keep in mind that you're going to need more time to

navigate airports, hotels, and tourist sites, so schedule extra time for everything you do so you're not rushed and put yourself into danger trying to rush to places.

10. Keep vital travel documents where they are easily accessible in a fanny pack. Bring extra $1 bills so that you can tip the attendants and anyone who helps facilitate your journey.

11. Be cool; stress, pain, and discomfort can be magnified by the fatigue of traveling, so remember to stay calm and courteous to others.

If you run into access-related problems while at the airport, ask to speak to the Complaints Resolution Official (CRO); all airlines in the US are required to have a CRO on duty during airport operating hours. This airline employee is specially trained in the ACAA and can resolve access-related issues on the spot.

If the CRO is unable to assist you, file a written complaint with the airline after you return home. Sometimes this can be your best and only option for receiving monetary compensation for damages. Be mindful of deadlines, as airlines are not required to respond to complaints postmarked more than forty-five days after the incident. For complaints filed on time, the airlines must respond within thirty days.

If these two steps have not resolved your complaint, then you can file a complaint with the DOT for access-related problems. Claims must be done within six months of the incident and can result in changes to airline policies and practices. Filing a complaint can help make air travel more accessible.

I was fortunate enough to have the opportunity to travel in a wheelchair and on crutches. Some of the critical issues that quickly became apparent to me:

1. Be patient, as many people mean well, but not everyone will be familiar with your needs and limitations. Also, keep

in mind that most people are not patient, so they will avoid you or try not to help you, not always because they don't want to but because they are worried that they won't be able to provide the help you need. So, accept help where you can, and when people can't or won't, don't stress about it. Move on to the next person, or take the time to educate the person on your needs and on how they can help you. Explain that even though you might not be able to do things the way others do you can still enjoy being there and experiencing it your way. So, avoid situations where others can take advantage of or cause you harm. I usually avoided exploring dark streets at night, brought a companion with me to dangerous countries, and used transportation to avoid moving through areas of higher risk. Don't allow fear to force you into staying at home, most people are conscious of people with disabilities. I've experienced extreme kindness from folks from all around the world. People who were helpful and went out of their way to assist me when no one required them to do so. Most people will respect and admire you for taking on the challenge and try to help any way they can.

2. Although I'm 6' 2", 210 lbs., and have years of experience in martial arts, I felt an immediate sense of vulnerability, and this is normal when you're in a wheelchair or on crutches. So, avoid situations where others can take advantage of or cause you harm. I avoided exploring dark streets at night, brought a companion with me to dangerous countries, and used transportation to avoid moving through areas of higher risk. Don't allow fear to force you into staying at home. Most people are conscious of people with disabilities, and I've experienced extreme kindness from folks from all around the world. People who were helpful and went out of their way to assist me when no one required them to do so. Most people will respect and admire you for taking on the challenge and try to help however they can.

Nonetheless, you must be aware of your limitations and avoid situations where you could be at a significant disadvantage. Try to join groups, inquire before. Avoid dangerous areas. Stay away from lonely or dimly lit places.

Don't accept private rides or tours from strangers. When you go out, inform the hotel staff of your plans and anticipated return time. I'd also recommend checking in with someone at home regularly so they are aware of where you are in case you need assistance.

3. Be conservative with your plans, and don't try to pack too many activities into one day. It's best to leave extra time for completing the activities, so you're not under time constraints, since you won't be able to complete them as you usually would. Most things are going to take longer than they usually do, because you're going to have to wait for elevators, assistance from staff, and you're going to need extra rest breaks.

4. Allow extra time for sleep and recovery. Typically, when I travel, I can stay on my feet for up to sixteen hours a day walking and sightseeing, but while in a wheelchair or on crutches, a few hours were often enough to leave me exhausted. Remember, your body is meant to move you around most efficiently while on two legs. If you're using your arms to propel a wheelchair, you have a battery-powered wheelchair, or have to use your shoulders and arms to move you around on a pair of crutches; you're going to be moving in a much less efficient manner than a person normally would, and you're going to be expending much more energy as well. Give yourself extra time to sleep and take breaks throughout the day, so you don't exert yourself too much and cause yourself to get tendonitis, strains, or muscle tears. As mentioned before, make sure you prepare for your trip by spending extra time mobilizing yourself and preparing your body for the extra endurance needed to travel.

5. Start with more comfortable travel destinations until you get up to speed. Being stuck inside for months on end can be boring and depressing, but I was unsure of how to proceed because I felt vulnerable. So, I started with road trips in the western USA with my cousin Miska. I was unable to drive because of all the hardware installed in my body, and I needed help unloading my wheelchair; therefore, Miska drove, and I was the passenger. As my

endurance and travel know-how increased, we went to first-world destinations like Hawaii. As my mobility improved, even more, I set out solo with crutches to countries such as Mexico, and I used a walking cane in the jungles of Suriname, Guyana, and French Guiana. As you experience early success in your travels, you will slowly work out the bugs, develop strategies, and gain confidence in how to do things.

6. Use social media to connect with other people with limited mobility, who live at the travel destinations you'd like to visit, and get ideas about strategies you can use to navigate the local environment.

7. Know that it is typical for a person with limited mobility to have to pay more for tours and other services. You are going to require more time and effort from the hosts, so don't be taken aback when you hear they may be charging you more than others. It's not personal; it's economics, so don't let that be a deterrent to engaging in activities. You never know when or if you'll have the opportunity to experience something special.

Chapter 18.

Insurance

Lowrider Car Show Elysian Park California

Rental Car Insurance

It's always recommended to have some form of insurance when you rent a car to avoid unnecessary risks. Start by calling and speaking with an agent at your credit card company and your car insurance company to find out what types of car rental coverage they provide. Using both of these options to start with, will allow you to use something you already have so you don't have the added travel expense.

If you're in an accident, your liability insurance will only pay up to your policy limits for the damages to other cars or property. Collision coverage on your regular policy would pay for accident-related costs to a rental car. Your comprehensive coverage would cover damages to the rental vehicle not related to a traffic accident, such as theft or vandalism.

Most policies have some exclusions; such as, not covering cars rented outside your country, covering vehicles only for leisure (not business), offering only secondary coverage (not primary), and not covering luxury vehicles. So be aware of all exclusions and applicable deductibles so you can get additional insurance if needed to cover those gaps.

Credit cards give some form of rental car insurance coverage. But they don't cover personal injury or personal liability, although you may have that coverage through your auto insurance and health insurance. But they do typically cover collision damage and theft protection. Credit card coverage is secondary, which means they'll cover whatever your car insurance doesn't cover. Possibly including paying for your deductible, towing charges, and other fees. Credit card companies also have restrictions and exclusions. They may not include some fees or offer coverage in certain countries.

Once you figure out what limitations your insurance policy and your credit card have, you'll decide whether or not to buy more coverage to cover the gaps. You can either buy it from the car rental company or decline it and buy your own separate rental car insurance policy, called a standalone policy. The three most commonly used options are popular Allianz, Bonzah, and Insure My Rental Car.

Buying car insurance through the rental car company is the most convenient option, but also the most expensive and costs up to $40 per day for coverage. If you don't have another option, it's best to buy rental car insurance through your rental car company, rather than going without insurance.

Different types of rental car insurance coverage.

Collision Damage	The CDW is a damage waiver that will

Waiver (CDW) or Loss Damage Waiver (LDW)	pay for all of the repairs to a rental car if it is damaged or stolen. The loss must happen when an authorized driver is operating the vehicle and during the period when the waiver is valid. It usually requires a deductible payment.
Personal Accident Insurance	Covers emergency medical transport and medical benefits of the renter or their passengers if injured in an accident.
Supplemental Liability Protection	Car insurers are required to provide a limited amount of liability coverage, but you can buy a supplemental amount of liability protection to protect you from lawsuits. Liability coverage in your policy is meant to cover the rental agency and not necessarily you.
Personal Effects Coverage	Personal Effects Coverage will pay to replace up to $500 of your valuables per person. Make sure you know how your property insurance works first.

Car Insurance for Car-Sharing Services

Car-sharing services allow you to borrow a car from a neighborhood or your surrounding area for just a few hours. The largest US car-sharing service is Zipcar. Car insurance is included in your hourly or daily rate. Zipcar offers a combined single limit (CSL) of $300,000 per accident for drivers 21 and older. CSL is third-party liability coverage that covers the cost of injuries or property damage if a Zipcar member is at fault in an accident. Drivers get personal injury protection (PIP) for injuries that you sustain in an accident, and the Zipcar is also covered by comprehensive insurance. Car-sharing companies offer different levels of coverage, so check with the company for details on their coverage.

Insurance for Peer-to-Peer Renting

Peer-to-peer (P2P) car-sharing means that you rent

another person's vehicle, using applications such as Turo or Getaround. Turo offers vehicle owners their protection plans in case the car is damaged during the rental period. The policy covers physical damage up to the actual cash value of the vehicle, a replacement vehicle while the car is being repaired, and $1,000,000 in liability coverage. Check the policy coverage if you rent from a P2P company as coverage will vary, and many car insurance companies have excluded all types of coverage (liability, medical, physical damage, uninsured motorist coverage) if you use a P2P vehicle.

What to Do if You Get into a Car Accident without Coverage.

It's best not to put yourself in a situation where you'll need to pay out of pocket unnecessarily. Before renting a car, always call your credit card company and auto insurance agent to discuss how you're covered.

- If you get into an accident, first check if everyone is ok.
- Exchange contact and insurance information with the other party involved in the crash.
- Contact your rental car company and let them know about the accident.
- Call your own insurance company and ask if they'll file an accident report with the police or if you'll need to do that. Find out if the insurance company will cover anything and what the deductible will be. Your insurance company will only pay for damages if it offers first-party coverage. You'll be responsible for paying rental expenses for the length of time it takes to fix the car, so ask about those fees.

Travel Insurance

I generally don't recommend travel insurance. In most cases, you will be over-insured and wasting your money. Travel insurance is best used when your pre-paid and non-refundable expenses are more than you are willing to lose. For example, if you have medical concerns, then it may make sense. If you made a substantial financial investment in your trip and you have frequent health emergencies, then it would make sense to buy it. Just be aware of the multiple exclusions travel insurance has for canceled flights, interrupted trips, lost bags, delayed trips, or medical expenses. Enough loopholes, which make it hard even to cover your trip at a reasonable cost. If you can afford to lose the money invested in your journey, skip the travel insurance.

Some credit cards also offer limited travel insurance for your bags, missed flights, or even insurance for rental cars. A friend of mine had booked a flight with his partner a few days before the trip. Then his partner got very sick and was unable to travel due to a perforated bowel. They had no insurance, but they called the airline anyway. It turned out they got their money back for the airplane tickets, because they had bought them with MasterCard and had some travel insurance included in their purchases. This allowed them to get a refund for the money spent on the flight.

Visa provides thirty days of coverage for a rental car (check your card agreement for specifics), and MasterCard offers fifteen days. I have rented dozens of vehicles all over the world and have never had an accident or caused any damage until I went to Africa. I rented a car for thirty days. It was broken into three times in South Africa. By the time I returned it, the bumper had fallen off due to a large pothole in the ground. I rented another car and got a fresh thirty-day insurance coverage period on another credit card. The vehicle I returned had three broken windows covered with duct tape and cardboard, and a bumper that was being held on with zip ties. I was ready to find out if this Visa insurance really worked since I had declined all the coverage the rental car agency offered.

And in fact, it did. The rental car company charged me about $6,500 for the damages to my credit card, but it was repaid to me by Visa at no additional cost. The collision damage waiver (CDW) insurance usually sold by rental car agencies would have cost me $45 a day or $1,350 for thirty days. I had a rental car for two months so I would have spent $2,700 on insurance plus the deductible that is usually high for a rental car. If you get the CDW, then it usually voids your Visa insurance; you can't have both. It is an excellent service that Visa and MasterCard offer, but it is best to call and be familiar with how the coverage works.

Travel Health Insurance

Travel health insurance is different from travel insurance, and it is highly recommended. If you travel outside your country, your national health insurance policy, including Medicare, will generally not cover you. Travel health insurance is usually more affordable than regular health insurance and offers much more coverage. GeoBlue Travel Insurance is an excellent resource (geobluetravelinsurance.com). I have purchased their policies for myself and my parents, and have found that they offer coverage anywhere on the planet, and they are convenient to use and file claims. For about $30, you can get coverage for yourself for a two-week vacation. That's a fantastic deal considering the risks of incurring significant medical costs. Another option is the travel health insurance offered by American Express for its cardholders. The rates are about the same for the amount of coverage.

Working in hospitals, I have encountered countless scenarios where I have seen a family destroyed financially due to an accident or illness while traveling abroad.

I can remember two particular instances. One in which a young couple from Colorado went to Ecuador where the young man was bitten by a mosquito and got meningitis. He was treated in a hospital in Ecuador, but possibly due to lack of resources at the hospital, he ended up in a coma.

His girlfriend started a GoFundMe page to try to raise the $50,000 necessary to fly him back to the US so he could be treated here with better medical care and have the costs covered by his insurance. Unfortunately, the process took a while, and he ended up in a permanent vegetative state due to the delays. Had they purchased travel health insurance, he would have been seen at the best medical facilities there, and the insurance would have paid for a medical transport plane to bring him back to the USA for treatment.

Another patient who was under my care, a sixty-five-year-old male, who had flown to Mexico with his wife for a two-week vacation in Guadalajara, had a massive stroke while walking off the plane in Mexico. He fell to the ground with his bags in hand. The gentleman had ten grown children here in the US, all with their own children. Everyone pitched in to pay dad's medical bills so he could be treated in a quality medical facility and have a better chance of survival. According to the Mexican doctors, he needed three months to become medically stable so that he could be transported back to the US for treatment. At that point, the medevac plane cost the working-class family members $50,000 to get their dad back to Los Angeles.

Upon arrival in Los Angeles, the gentleman was brought to my acute rehabilitation unit for intense therapy. He made significant gains, although he had sustained a lot of damage from the stroke. I couldn't help but think how much better he might have been had he been brought in three months earlier, as his family indicated that in Mexico, he didn't receive therapy. They primarily had him in bed while he was treated. The family shared their stories of the financial hardship on all ten children, and even on the grandchildren who were able to pitch in. Three months of medical treatment and transport back to the US ended up costing them over $100,000. The entire expense would have been covered for about $40 in travel insurance. The risk/reward is too high to avoid not buying health insurance when you travel.

Chapter 19.

How to Save on Travel or Travel for Free

Become a Deckhand

Salvation Mountain near Palm Springs, California.

Join a crew on a ship in exchange for keeping someone company, being a deckhand, or for a particular skill you may possess. The captain of the vessel will give you free passage and often compensate you for traveling with them on their boat to their destinations. Once in different ports, you can jump from ship to ship and go just about anywhere in the world. Check out Find a Crew or CrewSeekers for postings from captains looking for crew.

During a trip to Puerto Rico, I met several people on the island of Vieques who were working in the restaurants, getting paid under the table and saving money to hitch rides on yachts and travel everywhere you could think of: French Polynesia, the Mediterranean, or merely the Caribbean islands. There were bars we would go to at night where the captains would post signs on the bulletin boards advertising that they needed deck hands with no experience to experienced. Some paid for their trip, some paid for room and board, others paid with labor depending on what skills they had.

Five Ways to Save with Travel Packages

A vacation package is meant to save you money by bundling tours, meals, accommodations, and transportation in one package price.

1. Put together your vacation package yourself without an agent. By using travel websites, you cut out the middleman, get the best price, and get what you want.

2. Try to bundle your hotel, flight, and auto rental all into one. The more options you bundle together, the more the discount tends to be. I've purchased packages that gave me my airfare for free, just for buying everything together at once.

3. Book last minute offers. Travel companies will start slashing prices on tour packages as the date nears. Often, they've sold some of the spots, and when there are openings, the tour operator faces the reality of either getting something for the seat or getting nothing. To fill empty spots, the tour companies will rely on deep discounts to clear inventory.

4. Try all-inclusive resorts. These resorts offer packages that include transportation, room, meals, and entertainment. If you're traveling in a group, these packages can save you on having to buy everything separately. They also tend to be high end, including steak and lobster buffets, and have some excellent entertainment options like Broadway musicals.

5. Stay longer and pay a lot less per day. Vacation prices

are not linear. If you play around with the dates, you'll find that the price drops the longer you stay, and sometimes the final average price can result in free nights at the all-inclusive resort or the entire package costing you less by adding more days. If there is a flight included in the package, that price is absorbed into your daily rate decreases as a percentage of the daily cost the longer you stay on vacation. Therefore, taking short trips, is often much more expensive than longer trips.

Cross Border Trade

I drove from Los Angeles to Panama, and at every border crossing in Central America, I found men at the border crossings waving fistfuls of dollars at me offering to buy my car for double what I had paid for it in Los Angeles. Due to their small market size, these countries have limited access to cars and other high-priced consumer goods.

Many entrepreneurs engage in cross-border trade transporting goods across national borders to explore new markets, access other customer bases, or take advantage of currency differences. Cross-border selling can involve various transportation methods, including driving, shipping, or air freight, depending on the nature of the goods and the distance involved. People sell used cars, farm equipment, clothes, cell phones, and almost anything else we have in abundance in developed countries sold for a profit in developing countries. Check with the U.S. Department of Commerce (Or the Department of Commerce in your home country) for the specific permits and documentation for each country.

I bought used Ford trucks in Los Angeles, loaded them with tools, clothes, and whatever else I could find on clearance, and took extended trips to Central America. Had I driven straight through, I could have arrived in two days. But I took the opportunity to explore for up to two months at a time along the Pacific Coast, surfing, sightseeing, and vacationing. At the end of the trip, I could pay for my entire trip and buy a one-way ticket back to Los Angeles from Guatemala or whichever Central American country I decided to end my trip.

To help ensure success on your trip, buy late-model pickup trucks, as those are the most popular vehicles in many developing countries due to the lack of good roads and the often-rugged terrain (it's also safer for you to navigate the streets in pickup trucks). Late model vehicles are also less expensive to buy, and it's easier to sell them for up to several times more than what you paid for them, as affordability can be an issue if you want to make a quick sale and continue on your journey. Also, purchasing four-cylinder American vehicles as gas tends to be much more expensive in developing countries, and large-engine cars are less desirable and have a lower resale price. American vehicles are also more affordable, and the parts are easier to access, particularly in the Americas. In recent years pirates have started popping up along the Pacific coast who are on the lookout for people driving from the USA with vehicles loaded with valuables to sell. So keeping a low profile, valuables out of sight, and moving on toll roads will help ensure your safety. As a bonus, toll purchases in Mexico come with auto and property insurance.

Craigslist, eBay, or Thrift stores are excellent places to buy used machinery, clothes, iPhones, or American cars. Once arriving at your final destination, you can quickly sell your items at the border crossings for a profit, but if you hold onto the things till you get to the city, you can fetch a higher price for everything at the local "Mercado al aire libre" similar to a swap meet. If you can, on crossing multiple borders, have numerous photocopies of your driver's license, insurance, registration, and title, as you'll be required to supply various copies of each document at each border to get a permit to transit in their country. Also, inform yourself of the requirements for returning the permit so you can enter the country again with another vehicle. For example, since Mexico has a border with the USA, it protects its domestic auto market by making registering foreign cars in Mexico difficult. They block anyone for several years from bringing a vehicle for tourism or any purpose into the country if you fail to return your pass upon leaving the country after a trip.

Get a Travel Rewards Credit Card

Using a credit card to pay for your regular ongoing expenses is an excellent way to build up free flights and hotels. Credit cards such as Orbitz Rewards Visa, Chase Sapphire, or the airlines' credit cards, allow you to build up credit for free travel and perks. Just don't accumulate unnecessary debt, or it will defeat the purpose of having the card. You can also join Travel Hack, and they will show you how to get free flights by accumulating miles with offers.

There are also tricks for how to best use miles to your advantage. Transfer miles within a partnership of airlines. For example, I needed to use 525,000 miles for a first-class round-trip ticket to fly on ANA to Japan from Los Angeles. Instead, I transferred 90,000 miles from Virgin Airlines to buy the ANA ticket. Since it was a partner airline, it only cost me about 17% of the actual miles for the same ticket. Using this strategy, you can transfer airlines within travel partners and actually get better tickets for fewer miles.

Eat for Free or at a Discounted Price

While on a road trip with the family, in a small town in Colorado, my mom had a breakdown because she was on a diet and was not allowed to have mayonnaise on her sandwich. She got upset and left my girlfriend and me behind.

As we wandered around thinking about how to get back home, we found a Salvation Army soup kitchen that was serving lunch. They offered the option to eat for free if you had no funds, or you could pay 50 cents for your meal. The food was very hearty, and we could eat as much as we wanted. We had spaghetti with marinara sauce, garlic bread, and Kool-Aid. We ended up calling my mom after she cooled down, and she came back to pick us up.

I had a similar experience in Atlanta, Georgia, when I was sixteen traveling with my friends to a baseball card show. We had run low on money, so we were sleeping outside the Convention Center in a nearby park until the show started the following day. We were on a very tight budget and found a soup kitchen that charged 50 cents for all-you-can-eat baked beans, garlic bread, and an orange drink. These places typically have discounted or free groceries you can take as snacks for later in the day.

In the USA, about 40% of all the food we produce is wasted and thrown in the trash. That comes out to over 150 billion pounds of food wasted and about $200 billion worth of food not eaten. So, if you're low on funds for food, don't hesitate to visit a food bank or soup kitchen.

Another option for fresh fruit while you're on the road is using Falling Fruit (fallingfruit.org). You simply add your location, and it provides a global map of sites where you can get free fruit from trees on people's properties.

Trade Labor at a Hostel

Hostels often welcome the idea of having international staff working there, especially if you speak English in a non-English speaking country. Trading labor for room and board is called "woofing" in the hostel world. Speak to the hostel manager and negotiate a deal for room, board, and even pay for your work. There are also websites like Hostelworld (Hostelworld.com) that have message boards and allow hostels to advertise job opportunities. If it's a country that requires a work visa and you don't feel comfortable working without a work visa, you can work for room and board so that no money is exchanged.

Ask for Travel Gift Cards

When you have a birthday or some other special occasion, ask for a gift card for airline travel, Airbnb, HomeAway from Home, or travel website gift cards.

My cousin Chris just graduated from high school, and instead of buying him something that'll end up in a landfill, I gave him a round trip plane ticket to anywhere in the world! His job is to learn the information from this book, work to raise the money for his travel, and travel alone somewhere in the world for as long as he can make his money last.

If you want to give a special gift to someone, provide them with an experience that they'll remember, rather than something that will eventually break and be forgotten. It can be a one-hour trip from your house, a bike ride, boat ride, or whatever you can afford. But rest assured these are the types of gifts that are never forgotten.

Work on a Cruise Ship

You can get paid and travel around the world by working as a staff member on a cruise ship. Check out Cruise Job Finder, CruiseShipJobs.com, and CruiseLineJobs.com. You can also contact the cruise lines and get gigs teaching classes depending on your areas of expertise: business, health, history classes, etc. Cruise ships offer educational lectures during the days for guests, and you can be a guest lecturer and in exchange get a free or discounted cabin.

Host an Educational Trip

Educational travel companies provide free trips for teachers to get them to host tours for students. Some will include a free training trip beforehand so that you can learn how to be a better guide. Some of the best outfitters include Explorica, EF Educational Tours, and CHA Educational Tours.

Drive Someone Else's Car Across the Country

You can either find someone who needs their car relocated on Craigslist, drive for a car rental company or Auto Driveaway, the largest vehicle-relocation company in the US. You need to be at least twenty-three years old and have a valid license. After putting down a $350 security deposit (returned upon delivery), you will be paid a negotiable rate (either flat or per mile), and gas will be charged back to the owner.

Relocate Motorhomes and Get Paid for It.

The usual cost may be about $200 a day for a recreational vehicle (RV) rental. However, most people rent them only one way, and someone else has to drive them back to the big cities, so RV rental places such as Apollo RV, or Cruise America offer deals where they pay you and all your expenses to drive the RVs back to desired locations where demand is higher.

My friend John regularly takes his kids on free RV trips, by helping the RV companies relocate their vehicles across the US.

Volunteer on Environmental Projects

You can look to environmental organizations for volunteer projects around the world, helping out with endangered species and the environment. One such group is Deadhorse Camp where you can work, get paid, and go on a polar bear viewing. Also, check out Go Global Expo for volunteer opportunities around the world.

Carpool or Hitchhike

There are multiple smartphone applications to help you hitchhike or carpool. You can either join others or have others join you to help offset the fuel costs. Some of the sites I use are the Waze Carpool application, Craigslist, and eRideShare.

Take Your Medical Skills on the Road

If you are a medical professional (doctor, nurse, occupational, physical, or speech therapist), you can go mobile and travel for free to places like Florida, Hawaii, military bases around the world and get paid for it. Companies like Med Travelers offer gigs everywhere that last from eight weeks to a year. The compensation varies based on experience, but traveling nurses or therapists can make as much as $15,000 a month, with food and housing covered. If you are a nurse or a doctor, you can also get free cruises and get paid for working on cruise ships for short or extended tours.

Teach English

You can get paid to teach English abroad for nine months to two years, and in some cases, have your travel expenses covered. Check out TEFL (tefl.com) for job postings teaching English. Another option is Diverbo that sends 15-25 English speaking volunteers to villages in Spain and Germany for weeklong trips to help locals practice their English skills. Diverbo doesn't cover your flight, but it does include your room and board.

Trace Your Ancestry

Israel, Hungary, Macedonia, Armenia, Cuba, and a few other countries have organizations that sponsor people to visit their homelands and learn about their heritage.

House Swap or Rent Out Your Home

I use HomeAway, Airbnb, and/or Craigslist to rent out my house, pay for my entire trip, and have money left over! Other options are HomeExchange, OfferUp, or Home Base Holidays. You have to pay a registration fee. These are usually an even swap, so they are not money makers. However, if you live in a place that is not a high rent area, this may be a better option for you.

House Sit or Swap

Craigslist has house swapping options available. HomeExchange, HomeLink charge an annual membership fee, but GuestToGuest is free and allows you to host guests in your home in exchange for them hosting you.

You can also house sit for family, friends, or check out MindMyHouse, HouseSitter, TrustedHouseSitters, Rover, HouseCarers.com, or other house-sitting websites that allow you to live somewhere else so you can travel.

Organize a Trip

Organize a trip for friends or family. In exchange for doing so, some travel operators will cover your costs if you function as a trip leader. YMT Vacations will give you a free vacation if you get twelve people to buy a trip from them; if eight of the guests book their flight through YMT, your airfare is also covered. Other companies that give you a free trip include Grand Circle Cruise Line, Select International Tours, All Aboard Travel, and Merit Group Travel.

Volunteer

There are volunteer opportunities everywhere in the world where you can get room and board in exchange for some type of service. Blue Ventures, Habitat for Humanity, United Planet, Volunteer Forever, California State Parks, WorkAway, WorkAway international, plus dozens of more organizations allow you to connect with people all over the globe to find volunteer experiences and to meet your travel desires. Archaeology Magazine also has opportunities to volunteer on dig sites around the world.

Volunteer with WWOOF

WWOOF (Willing Workers on Organic Farms) will offer you free accommodation, food, the opportunity to learn a few new skills, and immerse yourself in a new culture in the destination of your choosing in exchange for working on the farm. You will be responsible for covering your travel costs and a subscription fee of $75, but your room and board will be included. Another option is WorkAway, which offers cultural exchange all over the world.

Work in the Adventure Space

AdventureWork allows you to find short-term or long-term gigs teaching and working in facilities offering skiing, sailing, archery, and water sports in all kinds of sports travel destinations where the host can cover your expenses and pay you a stipend while you help out.

Study Abroad

Most universities offer study abroad programs for one semester up to several years. The cost can be less or more depending on the university you go to. Overall, the prices tend to be much less for students and often it's the same price as what you were going to pay anyway. This is an excellent way to experience being fully immersed in a foreign language and culture.

CouchSurfing

Couchsurfing connects you with people around the world who will let you stay in their house a few nights, so they can make new friends, practice a language, or get some help around the house.

Travel Blogging

Become a travel blogger or social media influencer and get free trips to places in exchange for your reviews, exposure, and endorsements.

Social Media Networking

Find friends and family whom you can stay with while traveling. This can be a mutually rewarding experience as many people are in need of increasing their socialization, like company, and enjoy the idea of having company over to show around.

Free Activities and Entrance Fees

Some museums offer free museum admission days, look for discount cards, coupons, and tourism cards. The best way to find out about these is to ask at your hotel, use the Groupon application, or just google the name of the place you want to check out if any discounts come up on the internet. Another suggestion is to use Craigslist or StubHub. I've been able to find private parties selling tickets to most places sometimes for as little as ten percent of the retail price. People sometimes get local promotional tickets and can't go, win tickets they're not interested in using, or simply have a change of plans, and just want to get what they can for their entry tickets.

If there are no other options, consider becoming a member of the museum. Sometimes if you're visiting in a group, it can be less expensive to buy a one-year membership than to purchase individual tickets for the day. Purchasing a membership will allow you to visit the museum multiple times a year, get a tax deduction, and use it to visit other museums for free through reciprocal agreements. These agreements allow members to visit other museums (sometimes in the hundreds) in different locations for free.

Free Bag Check

If you're going to be staying somewhere or you've already stayed there and need to store your bags, request to check in your baggage; most places offer this as a courtesy. If you're considering a location, you can check your bags in and inform them that you're waiting to hear from the rest of your party to possibly complete the reservation. If you don't end up staying at the location, you can go collect your bags and make sure you tip the bellman for holding your bags. The higher-end the facility, the more willing they'll be to accommodate you.

Join the French Foreign Legion

The French Foreign Legion (FFL) has been fighting in wars all over the planet since it was formed in 1831. They will accept citizens of any country, and you don't have to speak French. All you need is to buy your own ticket to France and have a valid passport.

The FFL accepts anyone with a questionable past, fugitives, criminals, and anyone willing to fight and die. You must be male and between 17- 39.5 years of age. You just show up at one of their eleven bases in France, and if you pass the basic mental and medical tests, you can start your five years of service immediately. You start with basic training, which lasts several weeks for physical and psychological hardening.

You get paid $1,350 a month; food, lodging, and travel expenses are free. The payoff is after three years of service; you may apply for French citizenship and can start your life over. If you get wounded, you'll automatically be offered French citizenship. You also get forty-five days a year of vacation. Check out Foreign Legion Info for more details on admission and benefits.

Chapter 20.

Create a Budget and Financial Plan

Creating and keeping a budget will allow you to balance your spending and saving to help ensure that you have enough money available for the things that are important to you and for reaching your goals. Budgets also help you stay out of debt, or help you get out of debt if you're in debt.

A financial plan tells you how to spend and invest the money you have budgeted to reach business goals. When driving somewhere that you're not familiar with, you use a map, or these days a mapping application, to get to your desired destination. This helps you get there the fastest, safest, and the most efficient way possible. Without a financial plan, you're going to waste money, make it more slowly than you probably could, and put your money at unnecessary risk. Create a budget with your current income and liabilities. Then make a written financial plan with short- and long-term financial goals that you can reference regularly. Having a business plan will give you a map to reference and to help you stay on the right path. It's like using a workout routine when you go to the gym; without a plan, you can get hurt from overtraining, or not get the physique you want for the beach.

One strategy to use is the 50-30-20 method. Senator Elizabeth Warren helped develop this plan while at Harvard. The biggest piece, 50% of your take-home income, should go towards essentials and basic living expenses: food, housing, and transportation. The second is 30% for flexible spending on discretionary expenses; clothing, travel, and entertainment. The last 20% goes towards helping you meet your financial goals of paying down debt and saving.

First, look at all your sources of income and determine

how much you have available to spend each month. This will be your total income and this is what you're going to divide up into your 50/30/20 budget plan. If you're self-employed, you'll need to track your wages more closely and base your plan on your average monthly income.

Second, keep track of all of your spending and divide it up into the three categories of essentials, flexible spending, and financial goals. Now, if you're overspending in one of the categories, adjust it so you're falling into the 50/30/20 parameters.

For example, if you're making $3,000 a month, your budget should be $1,500 for essentials, $900 for flexible spending, and $600 for financial goals. If you're spending $2,000 on essentials, then you have to cut it by at least $500. The easiest way to do this is by cutting the big three: transportation, food, and housing. One suggestion is to add a roommate who pays $750 a month, this way you're covering the extra $500 you went over on your essentials category, and now you have an extra $250 to go into one of your other categories, like financial goals.

There are several ways to save on transportation, like carpooling, riding a bike, or using public transportation.

Food is tricky because you want to save on the sources of food but not on the quality. For example, a friend of mine and his wife really wanted to buy a nice house so they started eating top ramen every day for a year. They saved a lot of money and bought a house. But I don't believe that the collateral damage from the high salt and low nutrition was worth it, because they ended up with high blood pressure. Instead, keep eating high-quality organic fruits and veggies, and cut back on eating out and substitute with economical options.

Overall the strategy is to cut as much as you can from the essentials and flexible spending categories so you can add more to the financial goals category.

The 50-30-20 Rule works, because it's simple and

everything is clearly defined, making it much more likely that you'll stick to your plan and meet your financial goals. It also allows you to adjust percentages to help you meet your goals faster.

For more strategies on building wealth to increase your travel budget check out these books: How to Become Rich and Successful. The Secret of Success and the Habits of Successful People. Entrepreneurship and Developing Entrepreneur Characteristics or How to Become Rich and Successful: Creative Ways to Make Money with a Side Hustle. How to Become a Millionaire - Learn the Best Passive Income Ideas.

Chapter 21.

How to Calculate the Cheapest Travel Destinations Using Purchasing Power Parity (PPP)

Ernesto held some of the millions of Venezuelan pesos he received in a large black garbage bag in exchange for $40. A year later, those same $40 would equal a semi-truck full of currency after 8 million percent inflation set in.

The most common question people ask is, "what are the cheapest travel destinations." The simple answer would be to make a list of countries that you think are the cheapest according to what you feel is "cheap" by comparing it to your home currency. But that is subjective, and it only takes into consideration the money you spend. Therefore, other factors must be considered to answer this question truthfully.

A more comprehensive and scientific way to calculate cheap travel destinations is to use purchasing power parity (PPP). PPP tells you what value of goods your currency can buy, according to the exchange rate. For example, let's say you want to travel to Mexico, and you want to figure out if Mexico would be a cheap travel destination for you coming from the USA. You could start with something simple that is found almost everywhere, a can of Coca Cola. In the USA a can of Coke costs $1, while in Mexico it's 5 Mexican pesos (0.25 cents USD), this is a ratio of 1:5. Then you compare this ratio to the actual exchange rate, which is $1= 20 Mexican peso, a ratio of 1:20.

Another way to look at it is to convert everything into your currency. For example, the American would pay $1 for the Coke in the USA and $0.25 for the Coke in Mexico, while the Mexican would pay 5 Mexican pesos for the Coke in Mexico and 20 Mexican pesos for the Coke in the USA.

In other words, an American traveling to Mexico can buy four cans of Coke in Mexico for the same price he would pay in the USA. He could buy four times as much stuff in Mexico as he could buy in the USA. On the other hand, a Mexican traveling to the USA would pay four times more than usual for items in the USA than he would in Mexico or 25% of what he could typically buy back in Mexico.

The Mexican tourists should buy sunblock, clothes, snacks, toiletries, and anything else they might need for their trip at home before traveling to the USA.

The American traveler should go with empty bags and load up on everything he might need at a 75% discount in Mexico. He should fill his luggage with goods to bring home as well to benefit from the PPP.

Using these examples gives you a simple but very accurate way to figure out if you're going somewhere that is cheaper or more expensive for you, and how much you need to budget for travel expenses. You can check out the World Bank's website at

(https://data.worldbank.org/indicator/PA.NUS.PPP.05? view=map) to see what your currency would buy you in another country. Although the exchange rates are not updated regularly, you can get a general idea of how PPP works. I also suggest reading the famous Big Mac Study presented on The Economist website (https://www.economist.com/news/2019/01/10/the-big-mac-index).

This simple calculation will help anyone from any country figure out where the cheapest travel destinations would be for them.

Chapter 22.

Best Travel Applications

1. XE - Free currency converter allows you to calculate live currency and foreign exchange rates.

2. GlobeTips - will advise you on how much to tip in more than 200 countries. It also offers a tip calculator for easy math.

3. Tricount - for trips with friends, family members, or simply splitting the cost between groups. Tricount calculates shared costs and splits bills so you don't have to think twice about who owes what. Just enter your trip, currency, and invite your travel mates to join you. Each time someone pays for something, you enter the amount in Tricount and the app splits everything evenly. You can also snap and store photos of receipts in the app. At the end of your trip, it will show the balances of who owes who what, making it easy to settle up at the end.

4. Metric Conversions - this app makes easy conversions in volume, weight, temperature, area, and more.

5. TripLingo - will help you sound like a local abroad. You select a destination and download the country pack, such as France. The app will translate your voice into French, image translator, selection of key French phrases, Wi-Fi dialer so you can make calls from abroad (you must add the credit, starting at $10), tipping section, safety, and cultural norms to help you blend in. The phrase section has tabs on humor and fun, nightlife, and flirting, all of which you can download and access offline.

6. Speedcheck - lets you test your internet connection on both Wi-Fi and cellular networks, keep track of your speed tests and contribute your results to a crowdsourced map of Wi-Fi Hotspots that shows the speed of each hotspot. You can use the included Wi-Fi Finder to find Free and Fast Wi-Fi - in Hotels, Cafes, Restaurants anywhere in the world.

7. Google Translate - instantly translates 103 languages, words, phrases, and web pages. The app also allows you to translate any poster or printed text in real-time using the camera on your smartphone.

8. Hopper - tracks flight prices and gives you periodic updates on whether you should buy now or wait. It doesn't just tell you to wait to buy your ticket but gives you a date when the price will likely rise. You can book reservations through Hopper as well.

9. Kiwi.com - is used to book flights, hotels, car rentals, even activities, and tours. The app provides information on destinations, airports, how to find lounges, ATMs, and luggage storage during a layover. The Nomad feature, has flight itineraries mapped out for you in packs, like the Tour Europe option. This one has a customizable itinerary featuring the cheapest way to enjoy three to five nights in Barcelona, three to five nights in Amsterdam, and three to five nights in Paris.

10. FlightStats and FlightAware - allow you to get the latest flight information. Quickly access global flight status by flight number, airport or route, and watch the flight travel to its destination with the flight tracker.

11. LoungeBuddy - offers access to premium airport lounges around the world, regardless of the airline or class you're flying. When you create a trip in the app, it tells you which lounges you have access to based on the airports you'll be transiting through, as well as how to purchase access if you don't already have it.

12. Priority Pass - gives you access to more than 1,300 lounges and provides meal vouchers at select airport restaurants across the world. You'll have to pay an annual fee to be a member, and an additional fee to enter each lounge depending on your membership. Use the app to pull up the lounges or restaurants that you have access to, including photos, hours, amenities, and specific location information.

While on a trip in Jamaica with my friend Alasdair a

travel writer and international news reporter, he suggested I get an American Express Platinum card to use for my travels. At the moment, I thought, "No way" I'm a budget traveler; I don't need to pay $700 a year to hang out in first-class lounges. However, Alasdair is a pro and comes from a family of professional travelers. So I decided to try it for a year. Like many situations, please keep an open mind; this is one of the best travel tools available, and not taking advantage of it isn't very smart. On one trip alone, I used the first-class lounge at seven airports. The entrance fees vary from $25-$75 per lounge, and I can bring up to 3 guests every time I enter.

When I travel alone, I invite three random people in so they can have the experience since many people never buy a first-class ticket and never get to experience the first-class lounge. These cards have many benefits, including free unlimited food and drinks, often showers with towels and toiletries, unlimited Wifi, office space, sleeping rooms, sometimes massages, large screens, televisions, etc. Since you can self-check in within 24 hours of your flight departure, you can enter anytime within that time frame and start enjoying the benefits. All you have to do is show your digital plane ticket on your iPhone, and security will allow you to pass, and the lounge will allow you access. I use the lounge to work, shower, eat, and have a comfortable space where I won't have to worry about getting to a plane on time.

If you travel frequently or are planning an extensive trip in a group, this is an excellent way to upgrade your entire trip for a minimal amount. Most premium cards that offer this option also provide other incentives to make sure the annual fee is easily covered if you travel. Along with the other incentives offered, you can recover your $700 investment on one trip when traveling with three other people. Several premium credit cards (AMEX Platinum) offer free Priority Pass membership for all cardholders.

13. GateGuru - Comprehensive airport information on shops, restaurants, and other amenities in both domestic and international airports.

14. Timeshifter - helps you avoid jet lag before your flight takes off, and offers in-flight and post-flight suggestions. The app relies on neuroscience research about sleep and circadian rhythms to provide personalized recommendations for each traveler, taking into consideration your age, gender, normal sleep patterns, specifics about your trip, and travel plans. Timeshifter maps out when you should avoid or seek light, take a nap, or try to stay awake. It even tells you if you should consider supplementing with melatonin or caffeine.

15. SkyGuru - an app designed by pilots that provides weather and turbulence forecasts for the route you're flying. If you're fearful of turbulence or flying, it allows you to be mentally prepared.

16. Hotel Tonight - last-minute discounts on rooms booked the same evening or up to seven days (up to 100 in some markets) before your stay. Available hotel rooms are categorized by basic, luxe, charming, and high-roller. The app has features such as being able to save favorite hotels and scroll through reviews, user-generated photos, rewards programs, and the daily drop feature. The daily drop gives you personalized deals with a special price only valid for fifteen minutes after unlocked.

17. Roomer Travel - If you have to cancel a trip last minute, this app and website help people sell prepaid reservations to others who can use them, usually at a lower cost. It can help you recoup money that might otherwise have been lost, and it can also help you save money if you buy a reservation from someone who can't use it.

18. Hilton Honors - allows you to see a map of the hotel layout and tap on the exact room you'd like when checking in via the app. Options include: upper-level rooms, near the elevator, or a specific view (ocean or pool). Other features allow you to pre-order your favorite pillow type, request specific snacks and beverages (at an added cost), check out, view your points balance, and elite status benefits.

19. Roadtrippers - helps you organize your road trip.

Roadtrippers lets you plan out your driving route, book hotels, and activities along the way. The app is useful for finding interesting and off-the-beaten-path roadside attractions as well as cool restaurants and can't-miss landmarks you can bookmark.

20. PackPoint - The app shows you what to pack based on the length of your trip, the weather in your destination, and the activities you're planning. If you are using laundry facilities in your destination, PackPoint will allow you to account for washing your clothes and wearing them multiple times.

21. AllTrails - lists of trails for hiking and walking around the world with pictures, maps, and directions to trailheads. It helps you find the best outdoor places when you're in an unfamiliar area.

22. Culture Trip - an SEO-driven website that runs articles with headlines that start "The Top 10" or "The Best Places." Locals write the content, and the app lets you save articles to wish lists. Make your wish lists for each destination or theme you're interested in (Salsa, Snorkeling Spots, etc.), and you can save the Culture Trip articles for your reference.

23. GasBuddy - it helps you find gas by location and price either in real-time on your phone or via its website. If you can save money by driving a little farther down the road, GasBuddy will let you know. It's available in the US, Canada, and Australia.

24. Google Maps - the best travel app for exploring destinations in most parts of the world. You can plan trips, star attractions, group attractions together, or save your maps offline so that you won't get lost even if you don't have data on your phone. Google maps also gives you directions in different forms (walking, driving, public transit, or ride-hailing), with time and distance information included.

25. iExit - travel app for driving trips, tells you exactly what's near every highway exit. You can mark your favorite

chains, and the app informs you if there's one coming up on your route, including gas stations, ATMs, and restaurants.

26. Rick Steves Audio Europe - If you're planning a trip to Europe, travel writer Rick Steves has an app for European travels with dozens of audio files. Some give you background information on a particular city or region, while others are audio guides for navigating popular sites.

27. TripAdvisor - one of the most comprehensive online sources for travelers with background information about different cities and regions, plus highlights of what to see and do. It has reviews of hotels, restaurants, and activities, written by members of the TripAdvisor community, as well as photos from their travels, so you know what to expect before you arrive. It also allows you to make reservations for any of the previously mentioned services through the app.

28. TripCase - a free app that helps you organize your trip by making an itinerary for you. The itinerary can include flights, accommodations, rental cars, restaurant reservations, and more. To make an itinerary, you forward travel confirmation emails to TripCase, and the app organizes the information for you. When you open the app, a complete chronological lineup of your trip is waiting for you. You can also manually add details to your trip.

29. TripIt - helps you organize your itineraries, travel confirmations, flight itineraries, tickets, hotel and Airbnb booking info, rental car reservations, ferry tickets, and driving directions. It creates an organized itinerary for you by finding confirmation emails in your inbox and pulling out travel information. You also have the option of forwarding emails to it instead of manually entering details and sharing travel plans with others.

30. Meetup - is an app for interacting with locals and other travelers who have mutual interests or shared hobbies. The app shows you groups that are formed around particular interests in your city, including yoga, family-friendly

meetups, photography, cooking, wine tasting, hiking, cinema, and much more. You can join groups to get updates on particular events you may want to participate in, and the app can even help with networking, as there are many groups dedicated to business and technology.

31. Viator - specializes in tours and packages, from daily excursions to week-long adventures with transfers included.

32. Wanderu - allows you to search for buses and trains the same way you search for flights. You can also use it for flights, car rentals, hotels, Amtrak, Megabus, BoltBus, and other ground services.

33. Happy Cow - helps vegan and vegetarian eaters locate more than 100,000 restaurants, coffee shops, bakeries, farmer's markets, and grocery stores in over 195 countries around the world. The app also allows you to organize by gluten-free, cuisine type, read reviews, and get recipes on the app as well.

34. Triposo - allows you to download city guides, maps, and walks in your destination that works offline. You can also read about the background of the city you're visiting, weather, safety tips, what to see and do. Triposo also offers options for booking hotels, restaurants, tours, activities, and experiences in over 50,000 destinations.

35. Smart Traveler - specifically for U.S. travelers, you can see what visas and vaccines you'll need before traveling and where to find help if you need it during your trip. Register your trip on the app, which gives your information to local embassies and consulates in your destination. If there's any disaster or tragedy, the local embassy can contact you to see if you need help.

36. TripWhistle - maps your location and allows you to text or send your GPS coordinates or location easily. It also provides emergency numbers for firefighters, medical personnel, and police in nearly 200 countries.

37. ByPost - Postcard Creator.

38. Airline Applications - Upon confirming your travel details, ascertain which airlines operate your flights, primarily since specific journeys utilize multiple carriers. Once determined, it's beneficial to download their respective apps to your iPhone. The utility of airline apps extends beyond mere convenience; they transform and elevate the flying experience. Many grant the ability to check in advance (saving you on in-person fees charged by budget airlines), sparing you from lengthy airport queues. You can also bypass the need for paper by utilizing electronic boarding passes directly from your phone (another way to avoid being charged by budget airlines to print a paper boarding pass for you). These apps keep travelers informed, offering real-time updates on flight changes, delays, or gate alterations.

Moreover, they afford the luxury of selecting or altering seats and help unfamiliar travelers navigate sprawling terminals with integrated airport maps. For those drawn to entertainment, some airlines provision in-flight content through their apps, ranging from free wi-fi, free phone messaging, films, and series to music. When the flight is oversold, you'll also get offers to sell your seat for sometimes double what you paid in exchange for a later flight. Frequent fliers can track and redeem loyalty points, while others can manage bookings or even get upgraded seats. In today's world, where minimizing physical contact is crucial, the apps champion a contactless journey by decreasing interactions and handling shared materials. Beyond flying, they sometimes double as travel companions, providing leads on car rentals or hotel accommodations. In essence, integrating these apps into your travel routine not only ensures smooth operations but also amplifies the overall experience.

Chapter 23.

Virtual Vacations in Case you Can't Leave Your Home

Just in case you ever find yourself under quarantine or unable to physically travel. These virtual experiences are excellent options for the real thing when that real thing is momentarily out of reach.

Using virtual travel, you can indulge your wanderlust and allow you to visit some of the world's most famous sites, including natural wonders, works of art, and architectural miracles. Until your able to make the trip in person, you can enjoy exploring them from afar. More and more of the most visited sites are going virtual, so check out the websites for some of your favorite places for information. However, here are some of our favorites.

America's National Parks

The Grand Canyon

Grand Canyon National Park, located in Arizona, is one of the world's most famous national parks. The virtual tour explains the layered bands of red rock, revealing millions of years of geological history.

Hawaii Volcanoes National Park

Volcanoes National Park is on the big island of Hawaii. Take a virtual tour through the heart of the Kīlauea and Mauna Loa active volcanoes. Visit Crater Rim Drive, steam vents, and the Thurston Lava Tube (Nāhuku).

Yellowstone National Park

Yellowstone located mostly in Wyoming, Idaho, and Montana, is a 3,500-sq.-mile wilderness full of life. Hundreds of animal species, including moose, bears, wolves, bison, elk, and antelope roam the park. The virtual tours of Yellowstone include canyons, forests, hot springs, alpine rivers, and gushing volcanic geysers, including its most famous, Old Faithful. Check out some of America's most iconic parks here. (nps.gov)

Deep Ocean Dives

The National Oceanic and Atmospheric Administration (NOAA) is an American scientific agency within the United States that studies the oceans, major waterways, and the atmosphere. You can do virtual dives through National Marine Sanctuaries, such as the Florida Keys, the reefs of Hawaii, or the waters around American Samoa. Check out all the virtual dives here. (sanctuaries.noaa.gov)

Aurora Borealis

The aurora, also known as the polar lights, northern lights, or southern lights, is nature's most fantastic light show. A natural light display in the high-latitude of Earth's sky is the result of disturbances in the magnetosphere caused by the solar wind. Check out the light show here. (explore.org)

Monterey Bay Aquarium

Monterey Bay Aquarium is a public aquarium in Monterey, California. Famous for its regional focus on the marine habitats of Monterey Bay. Watch live streams of the sea otters, kelp forest, or Moon Jellies. Check out all the aquarium's here. (montereybayaquarium.org)

The San Diego Zoo

The San Diego Zoo is the USA's most-visited and is located in Balboa Park, San Diego, California. The park houses more than 3,500 animals of more than 650 species and subspecies. Visit multiple open-air habitats and learn about conservation science virtually. Check out the zoo's exhibits here. (animals.sandiegozoo.org)

The Metropolitan Opera

The Metropolitan Opera is based in New York City, in the Metropolitan Opera House at the Lincoln Center for the Performing Arts. It remains one of New York City's most important cultural institutions, and you can stream free encores of the past decade of performances. Check out the Met's performances here. (metopera.org)

Berlin Philharmonic

The Berlin Philharmonic orchestra is based in Berlin, Germany, and ranked one of the top orchestras in the world, famous for its virtuosity and compelling sound. Listen to the orchestra's Digital Concert Hall and take in hundreds of incredible performances from your home. Check out the Philharmonic's virtual concerts here. (digitalconcerthall.com)

Sydney Opera House

The Sydney Opera House is one of the world's most iconic buildings. It is a performing arts center in Sydney, New South Wales, Australia. The virtual tour accompanies the Sydney Symphony Orchestra through a typical day, to the setup and execution of world-class performances. Check out the whole tour here. (youtube.com/watch?v=_hunddVoMjo)

Vienna State Opera

The Vienna State Opera is one of the world's great opera houses, based in Vienna, Austria. The Renaissance Revival venue is now streaming operas and ballets. Check out the performances here. (wiener-staatsoper.at)

SafariLive

WildEarth's safariLIVE is an award-winning, tour guide

hosted live safari, broadcast directly from the African wilderness into your home.

Ride along with an expert ranger through unfamiliar terrain in search of the lions, leopards, hyenas, wildebeest, or elephants. Check out the safari's here. (facebook.com/WildEarthLIVE)

Most of the World's Top museums

The British Museum, in the Bloomsbury area of London, United Kingdom, has over 8,000,000 works and is one of the world's largest. Check out the museum's virtual tour here. (britishmuseum.withgoogle.com)

The Vatican Museums

The Vatican Museums include the Sistine Chapel in the Apostolic Palace, the official residence of the pope, in Vatican City. The 15th century Sistine Chapel is known for Michelangelo's ceiling frescos. You'll visit them virtually along with multiple Vatican Museums, Raphael's Room, and the new wing. Check out the Vatican Museum's virtual tours here. (museivaticani.va)

The National Museum of Natural History

The National Museum of Natural History is part of the Smithsonian Institute, and one of the world's most visited museums. Check out the museum's virtual tours here. (naturalhistory.si.edu)

The Louvre

The Louvre Museum is the world's largest art museum and a historic monument in Paris, France. Check out all the museum's virtual tours. (louvre.fr)

The Museum of Modern Art in New York City

The Museum of Modern Art is an art museum located in Midtown Manhattan, New York City, develops and collects modern art, and is considered one of the largest and most influential museums of contemporary art in the world.

Check out the museum's whole tour here. (artsandculture.google.com)

Check out some of the world's top museums here. (smithsonianmag.com)

The Taj Mahal

The Taj Mahal is a white marble mausoleum on the bank of the Yamuna river in the Indian city of Agra. A 17th-century Mughal emperor built this UNESCO World Heritage Site in memory of his favorite wife. Taj Mahal is one of the most famous structures on earth. Check out the whole video here. (youtube.com/watch?v=665AHTNpf2o)

The Great Wall of China

The Great Wall of China is over 4,000 miles long and over 2000 years old. It is a series of fortified walls built across the historical northern borders of China to protect the Chinese states and empires against invaders. Check out the tour here. (thechinaguide.com)

Versailles

Versailles, a UNESCO World Heritage Site, is a city in the Yvelines département in the Île-de-France region, known worldwide for the extravagant bed chambers, the pastel ceiling of the Royal Opera House, the Hall of Mirrors, and the renowned royal gardens. Check out the whole tour here. (artsandculture.google.com)

Street Art Tours

Street art is unofficial and independent visual art created in public locations for public enjoyment. You can explore some of the world's best graffiti, using Google's impressive Street Art collection. Check out all the exhibitions here. (streetart.withgoogle.com)

Chapter 24.

Top Ten Life-Changing Experiences

The Top Ten Most Interesting Museums in the World

1. The Louvre, Paris, France
2. The Smithsonian Institute, Washington, DC, USA
3. The Egyptian Museum, Cairo, Egypt
4. The British Museum, London, England
5. Auschwitz-Birkenau Memorial and Museum, Poland
6. The Metropolitan Museum of Art, NYC, USA
7. Museo Nacional del Prado, Madrid, Spain
8. The Kennedy Space Center, Titusville, Florida, USA
9. The Houston Museum of Natural Science, Houston, USA
10. The War Museum Korea, Seoul, Korea

The Ten Coolest Natural Experiences to See in the World

1. Bioluminescent Bay, Vieques, Puerto Rico
2. Catatumbo Lightning, Lake Maracaibo, Venezuela
3. Hearing the Indri Lemur in Madagascar
4. Seeing lava from Kilauea's eruption flowing faster than you can run, Hawaii, USA
5. Northern Lights, Iceland
6. Iguazu Falls, Brazil/Argentina
7. Watching Sea Turtles at Tortuguero National Park, Costa Rica
8. Seeing the most massive trees in the world, Sequoia National Park, California, USA
9. Listening to the sounds of the forest while taking a canoe ride down the Amazon River, Brazil
10. Watching fireflies, Great Smoky Mountains, Tennessee, USA

The Ten Coolest Activities to Do in the World

1. Taking an inner tube ride down the Mekong River, Vang Vieng, Laos
2. Taking a plane ride around Mount Everest, Kathmandu, Nepal
3. Snorkeling in the Red Sea, Dahab, Egypt
4. Taking a class with the Dalai Lama, McLeod Ganj, Dharamsala, India
5. Doing things backward at the Equator, Ciudad Mitad del Mundo, Ecuador
6. Seeing the Big Five in Kruger National Park, South Africa
7. Going to the demilitarized zone (DMZ), Korea
8. Shark cage diving, Cape Town, South Africa
9. Driving the Golden Circle, Iceland
10. The Mystery Spot, Santa Cruz, California, USA

The Ten Coolest Ancient Wonders

1. The Pyramids of Giza, Egypt
2. Bagan, Myanmar
3. Angkor Wat, Cambodia
4. Borobudur, Indonesia
5. Teotihuacán, Mexico City
6. The Colosseum and the Forum, Rome, Italy
7. Nazca Lines, Peru
8. Tiger's Nest Monastery, Bhutan
9. Stonehenge, Salisbury, England
10. Tulum, Mexico

The Ten Coolest Cities to Visit

1. Paris, France
2. Los Angeles, USA
3. New York City, USA
4. Mexico City, Mexico
5. Bangkok, Thailand
6. Tokyo, Japan
7. Florence, Italy
8. Rome, Italy
9. Marrakesh, Morocco
10. Hong Kong, China

Ten Habits of a Professional Traveler

1. Don't make assumptions
2. Be cool
3. Don't take things personally
4. Be honest
5. Try your best
6. Be flexible
7. Enjoy
8. Be careful with your words
9. Plan, be prepared
10. Be skeptical, but learn to listen before you judge

Top Ten Places to Visit That Have a High Concentration of Cool Stuff to Do

1. New York, New York
2. Paris, France
3. Cairo, Egypt
4. Rome, Italy
5. Israel
6. California
7. Florida
8. Puerto Rico
9. Madagascar
10. Iceland

Top Ten Places to Eat a Variety of Good Street Food

1. Bangkok street food vendors
2. Hong Kong street food vendors
3. Mexico City street food vendors
4. Los Angeles food truck vendors
5. Marrakesh, Morocco, street food vendors
6. Istanbul, Turkey, street food vendors
7. New York, NY, street food vendors
8. Saigon, Vietnam, street food vendors
9. Paris, France
10. Rome, Italy

Top Ten Places to Buy Interesting Souvenirs

1. Bangkok, Thailand,

2. Tijuana, Mexico
3. New Delhi, India
4. Hollywood, California
5. Marrakesh, Morocco
6. Florence, Italy
7. West Bank, Palestine
8. Beijing, China
9. Dar Es Salaam, Tanzania
10. Cairo, Egypt

Top Ten Road Trips in the World

1. The Pacific Coast Highway, California, USA
2. Route 66, multiple states, USA
3. The Ring Road, Iceland
4. Amalfi Coast, Italy
5. The Wild Atlantic Way, Ireland
6. North Coast 500, Scotland
7. The Mexican Pacific Coast from Mazatlán to Chiapas, Mexico
8. The Baja California Highway from Tijuana to Cabo San Lucas, Mexico
9. Cancún to Panamá, México and Central América
10. Orlando to Key West, Florida, USA

Top Ten Dance Destinations

1. Havana, Cuba
2. Cali, Colombia
3. Las Vegas, Nevada
4. New York, New York
5. Berlin, Germany
6. Jakarta, Indonesia
7. Los Angeles, California
8. Miami, Florida
9. Bangkok, Thailand
10. Ibiza, Spain

Best Travel Agency Websites

Booking

The world's most comprehensive website for everything from the hotel to airfare, it's also available in more than 40 languages and operates in 207 countries, the best travel site for packages.

Last Minute

The best travel sites for all-inclusive vacations if you decide to go on a last-minute trip. This site also has payment plans, extra entertainment bookings, and gift cards.

Expedia

Expedia has the most extensive rewards program with exclusive discounts on hotels, cars, luxury travel, and packages. The variety of offerings has made Expedia one of the most popular travel sites.

Hotwire

This website has some of the best bundle pricing. Book a "Hot Rate" flight if your travel plans are flexible. You won't know your exact flight time or which airline you're on until after you book, but you'll find the best prices. The Hotwire application gets you the lowest prices.

Best Travel Websites

Scott's Cheap Flights

This unique website tracks flights and their prices. If prices change, it emails you information that helps you save, including on first-class and business flights.

Kayak

Kayak has deals on complete packages, restaurants, cruises, hotels, rental cars, and flights.

Tripadvisor

Tripadvisor is an all-in-one website with information and reviews to help you with booking. The travel forum allows you to ask questions and find answers to specific questions regarding any destination.

Priceline

Priceline has some of the best last-minute deals, and the "Bundle and save" option for hotels, flights, cruises, and rental cars help you save tons.

Priceline offers some of the best last-minute hotel deals, with options like the discount finder, alerts when properties have lower-than-average prices, and showcases express deals and price breakers.

Orbitz

Orbitz can cover most of your travel needs and has a rewards program.

Best Travel Websites for Flights

Google Flights

Google Flights is a metasearch engine that allows you to search for low fares on multiple airlines, track prices, and book vacation packages and hotel stays. Once you find the flight you want, the website will send you to the airline's website to buy your ticket. You can also see price trends over specified date ranges.

Momondo

Momondo Flights is easy to use and has multiple tracking tools and mix-and-match fares.

Kayak Flights

Kayak allows you to search many different airlines at the same time. They also offer hacker fares that match two one-way tickets rather than one roundtrip, which is typically cheaper.

Skyscanner Flights

This site allows you to compare pricing and flight availability, then sends you the airline website to buy your tickets.

Skiplagged Flights

The best hidden-city flight tracker around. Hidden-city flights require travelers miss their connecting flight while on a layover. For example, I wanted a ticket to Paris, which was $900 OW from LAX. I found a ticket to Edinburg, Scotland, for $380 with a layover in Paris, so I bought that ticket and got off the plane in Paris.

Unique Travel Websites

GoGlamping.net

This site helps individuals "glamp" in safari tents, yurts, cabins, treehouses, and many other options.

UnusualHotelsOfTheWorld.com

The best site to help you find unique hotel accommodations for memorable experiences, it offers travel ideas, events, cultural immersion, and unique stays in igloos, treehouses, and caves, to name a few.

PrestigeOnline.com

Prestige lists 12 unique luxury sites worldwide, including underwater and capsule suites hanging from cliffs.

AtlasObscura.com

This site helps people plan small group trips to some of the world's most unique places. The membership option, courses, and expert guides help with immersion into the experiences.

BlackTomato.com

This site offers once-in-a-lifetime eccentric experiences, such as building an igloo in Greenland or walking with gorillas in Rwanda. This site can help you find the most unusual trips around.

Best Travel Websites for Hotels

Google Hotels

This site allows you to compare pricing and listings. It offers travel recommendations and gives neighborhood summaries. The hotel page is integrated with Google Maps so that you can type in "hotel," and your destination and results will appear on the map.

Kayak Hotels

Kayak shows multiple types of accommodations and total prices. It offers resorts, guest houses, rentals, and hotels.

Booking

Many other hotel websites belong to booking, but booking is the mother of all hotel websites. The site has filters for family-friendly vacations, types of accessibility for hotels, solo travelers, and different kinds of lodging.

Hotels

My favorite hotel website due to last-minute deals, a rewards program, and daily deals of up to half off hotels. Most hotels offer free cancellation, and most rooms allow you to pay now or later.

Group Travel Companies

Intrepid Travel

They specialize in unique experiences and sustainable, eco-conscious tours for small groups.

On the Go Tours

On the go specializes in travel groups for people over 40 and individuals who want to meet other travelers. Their individualized trips are all-inclusive, and they use only expert guides.

Exodus Travels

Specializing in travel groups for people over 50, they specialize in small group sizes and trips that accommodate different travel styles and flexible booking conditions.

Chapter 25.

Conclusion

Why do I travel? It's a multi-sensory learning experience where you can cram months of knowledge into one week. It's the only way to do so effortlessly. I studied for fifteen years, yet, I never found the intellectual stimulation that I get from traveling.

One day at work during lunch break, I sat with maybe eight physical and occupational therapists. My colleagues were all talking about how much they loved their jobs and how lucky we were to work there. I totally agree that being appreciative was the way to be, but one of my friends took things a step further. He raised his head and said, "I'm a lifer. How about you guys?" and several others joined in, "Yeah, me too."

They looked at me, and I was speechless; I was actually shocked to hear that. Here we had all just graduated within the last two years, after so many years of school. I figured we were all just starting out, and we were going to embark on all types of adventures. Instead, I was hearing that this was it, that we would merely be doing the same thing, in the same place, with the same people for the rest of our working careers. That did not sit well with me, and I could not imagine a future that predictable for myself.

It made me want to quit my job and travel more, and I remembered sitting in a café in Marrakesh, Morocco. In the background, I could hear the sounds of sheep being herded around, the melodic sounds of the Arabic language, and snake charmers playing flutes to cobras. My nose bathed in the smells of over a hundred different spices on the spice table next to me. My mouth was watering as I munched on my delicious tasting falafel with fresh pita bread, tahini, hummus, fresh tabouli, and my "doogh," a buttermilk drink flavored with mint. My skin tingled with the feeling of my wool kaftan, the 120-degree sunshine, and the tiny specks of sand whipped against me by the light desert breeze.

Visually, it was a buffet of merchants bartering, cobras, camels, Bedouin traders, centuries-old medieval architecture, and an array of other people making Marrakesh one of the most unique places you will ever visit. All in all, my brain and body were being indoctrinated into a new culture. The intellectual/sensory experience was unparalleled. In school, I had to study topics whether I liked them or not, and it was active learning. Traveling is a passive learning experience. You just need to sit back and allow your brain to absorb all the sensory information around you.

Remember, no matter where you are, you're never lost. You are somewhere. Feel safe and at home, because you are where you are supposed to be.

ABOUT THE AUTHOR

Snowboarding in Big Bear Lake California

Dr. Ernesto Martinez suffered a near-fatal assault that changed the direction of his life. The experience helped him acquire a greater moral understanding and develop greater empathy for others.

Martinez is a Naturopathic Doctor, Occupational Therapist, and Investor. He also enjoys writing, publishing, traveling, blogging AttaBoyCowboy.com, and running his YouTube channel AttaBoyCowboy.

So be sure to check out his fun books, blog, and YouTube channel.

Martinez's work as a Naturopathic Doctor specializes in anti-aging medicine and complementary cancer therapies. He focuses on a whole-body treatment approach utilizing safe natural methods, while simultaneously restoring the body's natural ability to heal.

His work as an Occupational Therapist has allowed him to help people across the lifespan to do things they want and need to do to live their life to the fullest. His strong desire to mentor and help others has led him to teach, share, and help them live better lives.

As an Investor, Martinez has focused his training and business acumen on real estate. With a family history of real estate investing and extensive academic training, he has developed innovative strategies for building wealth from nothing.

In addition to his medical practice and three decades of investing experience, Martinez is making his impact on the writing and media field. Through his books, blog, and YouTube channel, he is reaching a broad spectrum of people and teaching them how to live healthier and wealthier lives.

Martinez has taught extension courses for the University of San Diego in topics ranging from nutrition and general health to leadership and business. He holds five associate degrees from Cerritos College, a bachelor's degree from the University of Southern California (USC), an MBA in economics and marketing, and a master's degree in healthcare management (MHCM) from California State University Los Angeles (CSULA), a doctoral degree from Clayton College, and over ten other degrees and advanced certifications in areas including lifestyle redesign and nutrition, alternative nutrition, assistive technology, sensory integration, neuro-developmental treatment, physical agent modalities, lymphedema treatment, and property management. He studied over fifteen years working his entire academic career and for several years attending two graduate schools on two separate campuses at the same time.

He is a huge fan of all sports, reading, and being on the road traveling!

As an entrepreneur, Ernesto is usually problem-solving business issues, writing, and learning to be a better person.

He enjoys spending time with his family and friends.

By far one of his favorite activities is practicing his Random Acts of Kindness, where he tries to do three acts of kindness for strangers a day.

Bonus

Top Ten Ways to Decrease Your Environmental Impact During Travel per World Wildlife Fund (WWF)

1. Go on holiday during the off-peak period to prevent overstraining resources; you'll also avoid the crowds.
2. Find out about places before you visit. You may be visiting an environmentally sensitive area; in which case you must take extra care to stay on footpaths and follow signs.
3. Don't travel by air if you can avoid it, because air travel uses up large amounts of jet fuel that releases greenhouse gases.
4. Dispose of any rubbish responsibly; it can be hazardous to wildlife.
5. Use public transportation, cycle or walk instead of using a car.
6. Use facilities and trips run by local people whenever possible.
7. Don't be tempted to touch wildlife and disturb habitats whether on land, at the coast, or underwater.
8. Be careful what you choose to bring home as a holiday souvenir. Many species from coral and conch shells to elephants and alligators are endangered because they are killed for curios or souvenirs.
9. Don't dump chemicals into the environment; it can be very dangerous for wildlife.
10. Boats and jet-skis create noise and chemical pollution that is very disturbing to wildlife; don't keep the engine running unnecessarily

Top Ten Ways to Decrease Your Environmental Impact after Travel per WWF

1. Completely turn off equipment like televisions and stereos when you're not using them.
2. Choose energy-efficient appliances and light bulbs.
3. Save water: some simple steps can go a long way in saving water, like turning off the tap when you are

brushing your teeth or shaving. Try to collect the water used to wash vegetables and salad to water your houseplants.

4. Lower your shades or close your curtains on hot days, to keep the house fresh and reduce the use of electric fans or air-conditioning.
5. Let clothes dry naturally.
6. Keep lids on pans when cooking to conserve energy.
7. Use rechargeable batteries.
8. Call your local government to see if they have a disposal location for used batteries, glass, plastics, paper, or other wastes.
9. Don't use "throwaway" products like paper plates and napkins or plastic knives, forks, and cups.
10. Send electronic greetings over email instead of paper cards.

Top Ten Ways to Decrease Your Environmental Impact in the Garden per WWF

1. Collect rainwater to water your garden.
2. Water the garden early in the morning or late in the evening. Water loss is reduced due to evaporation. Don't over-water the garden. Water only until the soil becomes moist, not soggy.
3. Explore water-efficient irrigation systems. Sprinkler irrigation and drip irrigation can be adapted to garden situations.
4. Make your garden lively, plant trees, and shrubs that will attract birds. You can also put up bird nest boxes with food.
5. Put waste to work in your garden, sweep the fallen leaves and flowers into flowerbeds, or under shrubs. Increasing soil fertility and also reduce the need for frequent watering.
6. If you have little space in your garden, you could make a compost pit to turn organic waste from the kitchen and garden to soil-enriching manure.
7. Plant local species of trees, flowers, and vegetables.
8. Don't use chemicals in the garden, as they will eventually end up in the water systems and can upset the delicate balance of life cycles.

9. Organic and environmentally friendly fertilizers and pesticides are available - organic gardening reduces pollution and is better for wildlife.
10. Buy fruit and vegetables that are in season to help reduce enormous transport costs resulting from importing products and, where possible, choose locally produced food.

Top Ten Ways to Reduce, Reuse, and Recycle per WWF

1. Use email to stay in touch, including cards, rather than faxing or writing.
2. Share magazines with friends and pass them on to the doctor, dentist, or local hospital for their waiting rooms.
3. Use recyclable paper to make invitation cards, envelopes, letter pads, etc. if you can.
4. Use washable nappies instead of disposables, if you can.
5. Recycle as much as you can.
6. Give unwanted clothes, toys, and books to charities and orphanages.
7. Store food and other products in containers rather than foil and plastic wrap.
8. When buying fish, look out for a variety of non-endangered species, and buy local fish if possible.
9. Bring your bags to the grocery and refuse plastic bags that create so much waste.
10. Look for products that have less packaging.

Top Ten Ways to Reduce Your Environmental Impact at Work per WWF

1. Always use both sides of a sheet of paper.
2. Use printers that can print on both sides of the paper; try to look into this option when replacing old printers.
3. Use the back of a draft or unwanted printout instead of notebooks. Even with a double-sided printer, there is likely to be plenty of spare paper to use!
4. Always ask for and buy recycled paper if you can, for your business stationery, and to use it in your

printers.

5. Switch off computer monitors, printers, and other equipment at the end of each day. Always turn off your office light and computer monitor when you go out for lunch or to a meeting.

6. Look for power-saving alternatives like LED light bulbs, motion-sensing to control the lighting, LED computer monitors, etc. Prioritize buying or replacing equipment and appliances with their higher Energy Rating alternatives.

7. Contact your energy provider and what they offer in the way of green energy alternatives. You could install solar panels to reduce reliance on energy providers if they're slow on the green energy uptake.

8. Carpool. Ask your workmates that live nearby if they'd be happy to share rides with you.

9. Be smarter with your company vehicles. When reviewing your fleet, spend some time researching more efficient cars.

10. Clean and maintain regularly equipment to extend their useful life and avoid having to replace them. Just like getting your vehicle serviced regularly, your floors, kitchens, equipment, and bathrooms all need regular attention to protect their form and function.

Made in United States
Orlando, FL
11 December 2024

55399044R00148